1000 HEBREW SENTENCES:

Dual Language Hebrew-English Interlinear & Parallel Text

HEBREW BOOKS AND AUDIO BY L2 PRESS

HEBREW SHORT STORIES: Dual Language Hebrew-English, Interlinear & Parallel Text

HEBREW GRAMMAR BY EXAMPLE: Dual Language Hebrew-English, Interlinear & Parallel Text

1000 HEBREW SENTENCES: Dual Language Hebrew-English, Interlinear & Parallel Text

This series of three books provides over 5000 sentences of interlinear + parallel text
plus audio for maximum comprehension of every word and sentence.

1000 HEBREW SENTENCES:
Dual Language Hebrew-English Interlinear & Parallel Text

L2
PRESS

ISBN 978-1-952161-01-8

www.L2Press.com

First Edition

Table of contents

Introduction

D EAR LANGUAGE LEARNER: This book is intended for beginner and intermediate learners of Modern Hebrew who want to improve their Hebrew vocabulary, grammar, speaking, and listening abilities through massive exposure to one thousand wide-ranging sentences.

The sentences are presented in an *interlinear + parallel text* format for maximum comprehension of every aspect of the sentence. On the right side of the page is the interlinear Hebrew, romanization, and translation. Linguistically speaking, this is an interlinear gloss containing three lines of interlinear text: (1) the first line is the Hebrew source text; (2) the second line is the romanization, which improves speaking ability and provides a better overall understanding of the word; and (3) the third line is the translation, which gives more context-specific information than a dictionary possibly could. On the left side of the page is the parallel text, which is an English translation of the Hebrew sentence. The translation style of the parallel text is a free translation, whereas the third line of the interlinear gloss is essentially a literal translation.

A Hebrew audio file recorded by a professional voice actor is available as a companion to this book (available for purchase at L2Press.com). Audio files are important for developing correct pronunciation and listening ability. The second line of the interlinear is an excellent pronunciation guide, but there is no replacement for trying to emulate the pronunciation of a native speaker when it comes to developing a good accent.

How To Use This Book

Mastering the meaning, pronunciation, and usage of every sentence in this book will tremendously improve your Hebrew reading and speaking proficiency. Once you deeply understand this wide swath of Hebrew vocabulary and sentence structures, all future Hebrew-learning endeavors will be much more fruitful, reading native Hebrew materials will be far easier, and your speaking and listening abilities will be greatly enhanced. How does one master all of the material in this book? Here are tips to get you started:

1. *Extensive and Intensive reading.* Intensive reading is a way of reading a small amount of text in a detailed manner with the goal of understanding as much as possible while extracting new vocabulary and grammar. Extensive reading is reading quickly, for pleasure, without looking up anything, for as long as you want, with the goal of gaining massive exposure to the language.

   This book allows language learners at any stage to easily perform both intensive and extensive reading. If you want to improve your speaking abilities, then read aloud. If you aren't sure of the correct pronunciation, then look at the line below for immediate feedback and correction. And if you don't know the meaning of the word, look at the third line for immediate feedback and correction of the meaning. If you don't understand the meaning of a phrase or sentence, then look at the parallel text. This constant cycle of instant feedback and correction is a key attribute of deliberate practice and will accelerate your learning like never before.

2. *Active listening.* Written text with a corresponding audio file is a powerful combination of language learning tools. By hearing the language spoken, you can appreciate and imitate the prosody, melody, and intonation of the language. Combined, the audio and romanization will instill confidence, consistency, and clarity in how the language is spoken.

Prioritize active listening, which requires all of your attention and concentration, over passive listening, which requires little effort and yields minimal results. Productive active listening exercises include:

- *Shadowing*: listen to audio while repeating it nearly simultaneously, directly following the sound like a shadow. Ideally do this both with and without looking at a written version of the audio. Try to speak, as best as you can, like the native speaker, focusing on vowel sounds, vowel length, new consonant sounds, stress, and intonation.

- *Repeating*: listen to audio and then pause to repeat. Like shadowing, ideally do this both with and without looking at a written version of the audio, and try to mimic the native speaker as closely as possible. This technique, along with shadowing, is useful for developing a good accent.

- *Listening-Reading*: listen to Hebrew audio while reading English text. Following along in English while listening to Hebrew audio helps you understand what is being said. Can also combine this technique with shadowing (Listen to Hebrew, shadow in Hebrew, read English). This technique is great for developing your ability to understand spoken Hebrew.

- *Transcribing*: listen to an audio file while pausing frequently to write down exactly what you heard. Correct your transcription against the original text. This technique is good for *focused* listening comprehension.

3. *Spaced repetition with chunks.* Spaced repetition software (SRS) is an electronic flashcard system with a built-in algorithm that shows you the cards at optimal times for memorizing. If you are having trouble remembering certain words, phrases, and sentences after reading them many times, and you like to review flashcards, then put them into an SRS, such as Anki or Memrise, and review daily. "Chunks" are groups of two or more words that you should learn as a single unit. Chunks give you vocabulary, context, and grammar all in a short phrase. As an example, take the simple sentence "Last night I ate dinner with my family." Instead of breaking up the sentence into eight individual words and learning them all separately, it would be far more productive to learn it in three chunks - "last night", "I ate dinner", and "with my family". Now you know three chunks of words that work together and can be applied in new situations. "I was at my friend's house *last night*", "*I ate dinner* already", "I'm visiting New York *with my family*". Intuiting the grammar through context is more enjoyable and useful than laboring through tedious grammar exercises.

4. *Converse with a speaking partner.* In parallel to mastering the content of this book using the above techniques, find a native speaker and converse with them on a consistent basis, preferably at least one hour per week. The ideal practice partner is patient and will not simply correct your errors but will prompt you to self-correct. If you desire to speak fluently, there is no substitute for conversation practice.

Special notes about the Hebrew

1. There are no vowels points, or nikkud, used in this book. Instead, there is the romanization in the second line of the interlinear gloss. This was an intentional choice meant to get you used to reading Modern Hebrew without vowels points, which is the normal status of written Modern Hebrew in any situation outside of books for children.

2. The direct object particle את - *et* does not have an English translation and is therefore labeled "D.O.", for "direct object", in the third line of the interlinear. את is used only before *definite* direct objects and not

before *indefinite* direct objects. See the *Hebrew Grammar By Example* book for a more comprehensive description with examples.

3. It vs. he/she: Some Hebrew verbs are conjugated in reference to words with obvious grammatical gender, such as "he", "she", etc, but sometimes the same Hebrew verb is conjugated in reference to no word in particular. In this second case, the English translation provided in the interlinear uses "it" + verb. For example, in the sentence הוא נראה עייף - *hu nire ayef* - he seems tired, the verb נראה clearly is conjugated in reference to הוא. But in the sentence נראה שצדקת - *nire shetsadakta* - it seems that you were right, נראה is translated in the interlinear as "it seems", as opposed to "he seems".

Alphabet and Pronunciation

The Hebrew Alphabet and Romanization			
Letter[1]	Pronunciation[2]	IPA[3]	Romanization[4]
א	<u>a</u>lef	*takes vowel sound or silent*	
ב	bet	/b/ or /v/	b/v
ג	gimel	/g/	g
ד	<u>da</u>let	/d/	d
ה	he	/h/	h
ו	vav	/v/	v/o/u
ז	<u>za</u>'in	/z/	z
ח	khet	/χ/	kh
ט	tet	/t/	t
י	yud	/j/	y/i
כ	kaf	/k/ or /χ/	k/kh
ך	kaf sofit	/χ/	kh
ל	<u>la</u>med	/l/	l
מ	mem	/m/	m
ם	mem sofit	/m/	m
נ	nun	/n/	n
ן	nun sofit	/n/	n
ס	<u>sa</u>mekh	/s/	s
ע	<u>a</u>'in	*takes vowel sound or silent*	
פ	pe	/p/ or /f/	p/f
ף	pe sofit	/f/	f
צ	<u>tsa</u>di	/t͡s/	ts
ץ	<u>tsa</u>di sofit	/t͡s/	ts
ק	kuf	/k/	k
ר	resh	/ʁ/	r
ש	shin	/ʃ/ or /s/	sh/s
ת	tav	/t/	t

(1) The first column lists the Hebrew letters in alphabetical order, including the five special final (סופית -*sofit*) forms, which are letter variations that occur only at the end of a word.

(2) The second column lists the name of each letter, as pronounced in Modern Hebrew.

(3) The third column shows the phonemic notation for each letter as described by the International Phonetic Alphabet (IPA) for Modern Hebrew.

(4) The fourth and final column shows the method of romanization as used in this book.

NOTE: In Hebrew, word stress usually falls on either the final syllable (מלרע - *milra*) or the penultimate syllable (מלעיל - *mileil*). In this book, any stress that does not fall on the last syllable is noted with an <u>un</u>derline.

Romanized Vowels and Pronunciation		
Romanized Vowel[A]	IPA[B]	Similar to this English sound[C]
a	/a/	f<u>a</u>ther
e	/e/	p<u>e</u>t
i	/i/	gl<u>ee</u>
o	/o/	gl<u>o</u>ry
u	/u/	fl<u>u</u>te
ai	/aɪ/	<u>eye</u>
ei	/eɪ/	p<u>ay</u>
oi	/ɔɪ/	j<u>oy</u>
ui	/uɪ/	g<u>oo</u>ey

(A) The first column lists vowels used in the romanization of Hebrew in this book.

(B) The middle column shows the phonemic notation for each romanized vowel.

(C) The third and final column lists English words with comparable vowel sounds. The relevant vowel is underlined. Keep in mind that comparable Hebrew vowel sounds are shorter than the English versions.

NOTE: Double vowels, such as *a'a* or *e'e*, represent long vowels, which are common and key for proper pronunciation and clarity in speech. For example, מערכת - *ma'arekhet* not *marekhet*.

Representing Foreign Sounds with Hebrew			
Hebrew[1]	Sounds like[2]	IPA[3]	Romanization[4]
ג'	<u>J</u>erusalem	/dʒ/	j
ד'	<u>th</u>e	/ð/	th
וו	<u>W</u>ashington	/w/	w
ז'	mea<u>s</u>ure	/ʒ/	zh
צ'	<u>ch</u>ip	/tʃ/	ch
ת'	<u>th</u>ank	/θ/	th

(1) The first column of the table above shows some of the modified Hebrew letters used to create foreign (non-Hebrew) sounds. Aside from the double *vav*, which yields the /w/ sound, the letters are followed by a sharp apostrophe called a *geresh*.

(2) The second column lists example words that demonstrate the sounds created by the letters in the first column.

(3) The third column shows the phonemic notation for each letter as described by the International Phonetic Alphabet equivalent.

(4) The fourth and final column shows the method of romanization as used in this book.

1000 Sentences

(1) A big wedding with many people is our tradition.

חתונה גדולה עם הרבה אנשים היא מסורת אצלנו.

khatuna	gdola	im	harbe	anashim	hi	masoret	etslenu
wedding	big	with	many	people	she	tradition	for us

(2) A bottle of mineral water and two glasses please.

בקבוק מים מינרליים ושתי כוסות בבקשה.

bakbuk	ma'im	mineralim	ushtei	kosot	bevakasha
bottle of	water	mineral	and two of	glasses	please

(3) A family with three children lives next door.

משפחה בת שלושה ילדים גרה בסמיכות אלינו.

mishpakha	bat	shlosha	yeladim	gara	bismikhut	eleinu
family	comprising	three	children	they live	in close proximity	to us

(4) A friend of mine is a chef at a fancy restaurant.

חברה שלי היא שפית במסעדה מהודרת.

khavera	sheli	hi	shefit	bemisada	mehuderet
friend	my	she	chef	at restaurant	fancy

(5) A healthy diet is important if you want to live a long time.

תזונה בריאה היא חשובה אם ברצונך לחיות חיים

tzuna	bri'a	hi	khashuva	im	birtsonkha	likhyot	khayim
nutrition	healthy	it	important	if	your desire	to live	life

ארוכים.

arukim
long

(6) A horse walks into a bar, and the bartender asks, "Why the long face?".

סוס נכנס לבר, והברמן שואל, "למה נפלו

sus	nikhnas	lebar	vehabarmen	sho'el	lama	naflu
horse	it walks	into a bar	and the bartender	he asks	why	they dropped

פניך ?"

paneikha
your face

(7) A little exercise is healthy, but you should not overdo it.

קצת אימון גופני זה דבר בריא, אבל הכל צריך להיות

ktsat	imun	gufani	ze	davar	bari	aval	hakol	tsarikh	lihiyot
a little	exercise	physical	this	thing	healthy	but	everything	it needs	to be

במידה.

bemida
in moderation

(8) A mechanic is fixing my car.

מוסכניק מתקן את הרכב שלי.

musakhnik	metaken	et	harekhev	sheli
car mechanic	he fixes	D.O.	the car	my

(9) A new shopping center is being built here.

מרכז קניות חדש הולך ונבנה פה.

merkaz kniyot	khadash	holekh venivna	po
shopping center	new	it is being built	here

(10) A picture of my children is hanging above my desk.

תמונה של ילדיי תלויה מעל שולחן העבודה שלי.

tmuna shel yeladai tluya me'al shulkhan ha'avoda sheli
picture of my children it hangs above the desk my

(11) A recent study shows that pollution is still increasing.

מחקר שבוצע לאחרונה מראה כי הזיהום

mekh'kar shebutsa la'akhrona mare ki hazihum
study that (it) was performed recently it shows that the pollution

עדיין מתגבר.

ada'in mitgaber
still it intensifies

(12) A small band played at our wedding.

להקה מצומצמת ניגנה בחתונה שלנו.

lahaka metsumtsemet nigna bakhatuna shelanu
band small it played at the wedding our

(13) According to the weather forecast, it will rain tomorrow.

לפי תחזית מזג האוויר, ירד מחר גשם.

lefi takhazit mezeg ha'avir yered makhar geshem
according to forecast of the weather it will fall tomorrow rain

(14) Addiction to opioids is a big problem.

התמכרות לאופיאטים היא בעיה גדולה.

hitmakrut le'opiyatim hi be'aya gdola
addiction to opioids it problem big

(15) Adults must pay, but admission is free for kids.

מבוגרים חייבים לשלם, אך הכניסה לילדים חופשית.

mevugarim khayavim leshalem akh haknisa liyladim khofshit
adults they must to pay but the admission for kids free

(16) After the first half, our team leads 2-0.

בתום המחצית הראשונה, הקבוצה שלנו מובילה

betom hamakhatsit harishona hakvutsa shelanu movila
at the end of the half the first the team our it leads

2-0.

shta'im-efes
2-0

(17) After the meal there was a delicious dessert.

אחרי הארוחה היה קינוח טעים.

akharei ha'arukha haya kinu'akh ta'im
after the meal there was dessert tasty

(18) After we ate, we went for a walk.

אחרי שאכלנו, יצאנו להליכה.

akharei she'akhalnu yatsanu lehalikha
after that we ate we went out for a walk

(19) Ahmed came here to study English.

אחמד הגיע לכאן כדי ללמוד אנגלית.

akhmed higi'a lekhan kedei lilmod anglit
Ahmed he came to here in order to to study English

(20) All group members were present at the meeting.

כל חברי הקבוצה נכחו בפגישה.

kol khavrei hakvutsa nakhekhu bapgisha
all members of the group they were present at the meeting

(21) All the protests achieved nothing.

כל המחאות לא השיגו דבר.
davar hisigu lo hamekha'ot kol
anything they achieved no the protests all

(22) Always go to other people's funerals, otherwise they won't come to yours.

לך תמיד להלוויות של אנשים אחרים, אחרת הם לא
lo hem akheret akherim anashim shel lehalvayot tamid lekh
no they otherwise other people of to funerals always go

יבואו לשלך.
leshelkha yavo'u
to yours they will come

(23) Anything else? - No, that's all.

עוד משהו? - לא, זה הכל.
hakol ze lo mashehu od
all that no something more

(24) Are there any leftovers from dinner?

נשאר משהו מארוחת הערב?
me'arukhat ha'erev mashehu nishar
from dinner something it remains

(25) Are we going by bus or subway?

אנחנו נוסעים באוטובוס או במטרו?
bametro o be'otobus nosim anakhnu
by subway or by bus we drive we

(26) Are we going out tonight?

אנחנו יוצאים הערב?
ha'erev yotsim anakhnu
tonight we go out we

(27) Are we still meeting at half past eight?

אנחנו עדיין נפגשות בשמונה וחצי?
vakhetsi beshmone nifgashot ada'in anakhnu
and half at eight we meet still we

(28) Are you coming? - Of course!

אתה הולך? - כמובן!
kamuvan holekh ata
of course you going you

(29) Are you doing anything special this summer? - I don't know, we don't have any plans yet.

אתה עושה משהו מיוחד הקיץ הזה? - אני לא יודע,
yode'a lo ani haze haka'its meyukhad mashehu ose ata
I know no I the this the summer special something you do you

לא תכננו כלום עדיין.
ada'in klum tikhnanu lo
yet anything we planned no

(30) Are you for or against a ban on smoking in public? - I am for it.

אתה בעד או נגד איסור עישון במקומות ציבוריים? -
tsiburi'im bimkomot ishun isur neged o be'ad ata
public in places smoking ban of against or for you

אני בעד.
be'ad ani
for I

(31) Are you paying with cash? You can also pay by debit card.

את משלמת במזומן? את יכולה לשלם גם בכרטיס חיוב.

at meshalemet bimzuman at yekhola leshalem gam bekhartis khiyuv
you — you pay — with cash — you — you can — to pay — also — with debit card

(32) Are you sure that the library is open today? I thought it was closed.

אתה בטוח שהספרייה פתוחה היום? חשבתי שהיא סגורה.

ata batu'akh shehasifriya ptukha hayom khashavti shehi sgura
you — sure — that the library — open — today — I thought — that it — closed

(33) Are you well rested? We have a busy day ahead of us.

נחת טוב? יש לנו יום עמוס לפנינו.

nakhta tov yesh lanu yom amus lefanenu
you rested — well — we have — day — busy — ahead of us

(34) As soon as I know the date of the wedding, I'll let you know.

ברגע שאני אדע את התאריך של החתונה, אודיע לך.

barega she'ani eda et hata'arikh shel hakhatuna odi'a lakh
as soon as — that I — I will know — D.O. — the date — of — the wedding — I will inform — to you

(35) At home we often eat spicy food.

בבית אנחנו נוהגים לאכול אוכל פיקנטי.

baba'it anakhnu nohagim le'ekhol okhel pikanti
at home — we — we do out of custom — to eat — food — spicy

(36) At our company we make home furniture like couches and tables.

בחברה שלנו אנחנו מייצרים ריהוט ביתי כמו ספות ושולחנות.

bakhevra shelanu anakhnu meyatsrim rihut be'iti kmo sapot veshulkhanot
at the company — our — we — we make — furniture — home — like — couches — and tables

(37) At the moment there are no tables available.

אין שולחנות פנויים כרגע.

ein shulkhanot pnu'im karega
there aren't — tables — available — at the moment

(38) At the zoo they have 34 different species of birds.

בגן החיות יש 34 מינים שונים של ציפורים.

began hakhayot yesh shloshim ve'arba'a minim shonim shel tsiporim
at the zoo — there are — thirty-four — species — different — of — birds

(39) Be quiet. The kids are already sleeping.

תהיה בשקט. הילדים כבר ישנים.

tihiye besheket hayladim kvar yeshenim
you will be — in silence — the kids — already — they sleep

Before we go to the party, I want to change into a nicer outfit. (40)

לפני שנצא למסיבה, אני רוצה להחליף לתלבושת
lifnei *shenetse* *lamesiba* *ani* *rotsa* *lehakhlif* *letilboshet*
before that we will go to the party I want to change into outfit

יפה יותר.
yafa *yoter*
nice more

Biking on the sidewalk is not allowed. (41)

אסורה רכיבת אופניים על המדרכה.
asura *rekhivat* *ofana'im* *al* *hamidrakha*
forbidden riding of bicycle on the sidewalk

Bon appétit! / Enjoy your meal! (42)

בתאבון !
bete'avon
bon appétit

Both of my children have brown eyes. (43)

לשני ילדיי עיניים חומות.
lishnei yeladai *eina'im* *khumot*
my two children (have) eyes brown

Both the checking and savings accounts are free. (44)

גם העו"ש וגם חשבון החיסכון הם ללא
gam *ha'over vashav* *vegam* *kheshbon* *hakhisakhon* *hem* *lelo*
also the checking account and also account of the savings they without

עמלות.
amalot
service charges

Bye. See you soon! (45)

להת'. נתראה בקרוב !
lehit *nitra'e* *bekarov*
bye we will meet soon

Call this number in case of emergency. (46)

תתקשר למספר הזה במקרה חירום.
titkasher *lamispar* *haze* *bemikre* *kherum*
you will call to the number the this in case of emergency

Calm down, please. Everything is okay. (47)

תרגע, בבקשה. הכל בסדר.
teraga *bevakasha* *hakol* *beseder*
you will calm down please everything okay

Can anyone beat the world champion? (48)

האם מישהו יכול לנצח את אלוף העולם ?
ha'im *mishehu* *yakhol* *lenatse'akh* *et* *aluf* *ha'olam*
is it that anyone he can to beat D.O. champion of the world

Can I use your toothbrush? - No, that's disgusting! (49)

אני יכול להשתמש במברשת השיניים שלך ? - לא, זה
ani *yakhol* *lehishtamesh* *bemivreshet hashina'im* *shelakh* *lo* *ze*
I I can to use with the toothbrush your no that

דוחה !
dokhe
disgusting

5

Can I get another blanket? I'm cold.

אפשר לקבל עוד שמיכה? קר לי. (50)
li kar smikha od lekabel efshar
to me cold blanket another to get possible

Can I have an appointment immediately? - Unfortunately that is not possible.

אני יכול לקבל תור מיידי? - לצערי זה לא (51)
lo ze letsa'ari miyadi tor lekabel yakhol ani
not that unfortunately immediately appointment to get I can I

אפשרי.
efshari
possible

Can I pay by credit card?

אפשר לשלם בכרטיס אשראי? (52)
bekhartis ashrai leshalem efshar
by credit card to pay possible

Can I print this on your printer?

אני יכול להדפיס את זה עם המדפסת שלך? (53)
shelakh hamadpeset im ze et lehadpis yakhol ani
your the printer with this D.O. to print I can I

Can I talk to you briefly?

אני יכול לדבר איתך רגע? (54)
rega itkha ledaber yakhol ani
moment with you to talk I can I

Can you call me again later? We are eating right now.

את יכולה להתקשר אליי אחר כך? אנחנו אוכלים עכשיו. (55)
akhshav okhlim anakhnu akhar kakh elai lehitkasher yekhola at
now we eat we later to me to call you can you

Can you help me? I can't lift the box alone.

את יכולה לעזור לי? אני לא יכול להרים את הקופסה (56)
hakufsa et leharim yakhol lo ani li la'azor yekhola at
the box D.O. to lift I can no I to me to help you can you

לבד.
levad
alone

Can you help your grandpa set up his new computer?

אתה יכול לעזור לסבא שלך להתקין את המחשב (57)
hamakhshev et lehatkin shelkha lesaba la'azor yakhol ata
the computer D.O. to set up your to grandpa to help you can you

החדש שלו?
shelo hakhadash
his the new

Can you let me know by tomorrow morning?

אתה יכול לעדכן אותי עד מחר בבוקר? (58)
baboker makhar ad oti le'adken yakhol ata
in the morning tomorrow by me to inform you can you

Can you please speak a little louder?

אתה יכול בבקשה לדבר טיפה בקול רם יותר? (59)
yoter ram bekol tipa ledaber bevakasha yakhol ata
more loud in voice tiny bit to speak please you can you

(60) Can you please turn on the light? I can't see anything.

את יכולה בבקשה להדליק את האור? אני לא יכול
at yekhola bevakasha lehadlik et ha'or ani lo yakhol
you you can please to turn on D.O. the light I no I can

לראות כלום.
lirot klum
to see anything

(61) Can you take the dog to the vet today?

אתה יכול לקחת את הכלב לווטרינר היום?
ata yakhol lakakhat et hakelev laveterinar hayom
you you can to take D.O. the dog to the veterinarian today

(62) Can you turn down the volume, please?

אתה יכול להנמיך את הוווליום בבקשה?
ata yakhol lehanmikh et havolyum bevakasha
you you can to lower D.O. the volume please

(63) Carla spends a lot of money on her hobbies.

קרלה מוציאה המון כסף על התחביבים שלה.
karla motsi'a hamon kesef al hatakhbivim shela
Carla she spends lots of money on the hobbies her

(64) Caution! The floor is wet.

זהירות! הרצפה רטובה.
zehirut haritspa retuva
caution the floor wet

(65) Children are financially dependent on their parents.

ילדים תלויים כלכלית בהוריהם.
yeladim tlu'im kalkalit behoreihem
children dependent financially on their parents

(66) Children over 10 years old pay the full entrance fee.

ילדים מעל גיל 10 משלמים מחיר כניסה מלא.
yeladim me'al gil eser meshalmim mekhir knisa male
children over age ten they pay price of entrance full

(67) Class is canceled next week.

השיעור בשבוע הבא מבוטל.
hashi'ur beshavu'a haba mevutal
the class in week next it is canceled

(68) Coffee or tea? - I would prefer tea.

קפה או תה? - אני מעדיף תה.
kafe o te ani ma'adif te
coffee or tea I I prefer tea

(69) Come here so that I can show you something.

בוא לפה שאני אוכל להראות לך משהו.
bo lepo she'ani ukhal leharot lekha mashehu
come to here that I I will be able to show to you something

(70) Come in, the door is open.

תיכנסי, הדלת פתוחה.
tikansi hadelet ptukha
enter the door open

(71) Come, we'll sit on that bench over there.

בוא, נשב על הספסל ההוא שם.
bo neshev al hasafsal hahu sham
come we will sit on the bench that one there

Congratulations on the birth of your daughter.

ברכות להולדת ביתך. (72)
brakhot *lehuledet* *bitkha*
congratulations for birth of your daughter

Could you call again later?

אתה יכול להתקשר מאוחר יותר? (73)
ata *yakhol* *lehitkasher* *me'ukhar* *yoter*
you you can to call late more

Could you give me an example?

את יכולה לתת לי דוגמה? (74)
at *yekhola* *latet* *li* *dugma*
you you can to give to me example

Cut an onion into small pieces and fry it together with the meat.

חתוך בצל לחתיכות קטנות וטגן אותו יחד עם הבשר. (75)
khatokh *batsal* *lekhatikhot* *ktanot* *vetagen* *oto* *yakhad* *im* *habasar*
cut onion into pieces small and fry it together with the meat

Dad, can you help me with my homework?

אבא, אתה יכול לעזור לי עם שיעורי הבית? (76)
aba *ata* *yakhol* *la'azor* *li* *im* *shi'urei haba'it*
dad you you can to help to me with the homework

Day-to-day life is sometimes boring.

חיי היום־יום יכולים להיות משעממים לפעמים. (77)
khayei *hayom-yom* *yekholim* *lihiyot* *mesha'amemim* *lifamim*
lives of the daily they can be to be boring sometimes

Despite having the flu, I went to work, which was a terrible idea.

למרות שיש לי שפעת, הלכתי לעבודה, מה שהיה רעיון (78)
lamrot *sheyesh li* *shapa'at* *halakhti* *la'avoda* *ma shehaya* *ra'ayon*
despite that I have flu I went to the work which (it) was idea

גרוע.
garu'a
terrible

Did anyone witness the accident?

היו עדים לתאונה? (79)
hayu *edim* *late'una*
there were witnesses for the accident

Did you come by foot or bike?

באת ברגל או שרכבת על האופניים? (80)
bata *baregel* *o* *sherakhavta* *al* *ha'ofana'im*
you came by foot or you rode on the bicycle

Did you enjoy your meal?

נהנית מהארוחה? (81)
neheneta *meha'arukha*
you enjoyed of the meal

Did you get here by car? - No, I walked.

הגעת לפה ברכב? - לא, הלכתי. (82)
higata *lepo* *barekhev* *lo* *halakhti*
you arrived to here by car no I walked

Did you sleep well?

ישנת טוב? (83)
yashanta *tov*
you slept well

(84) Did you wrap your mother's gift?

עטפת את המתנה של אמא שלך?
atafta *et* *hamatana* *shel* *ima* *shelkha*
you wrapped D.O. the gift of mother your

(85) Dinner is nearly ready.

ארוחת הערב כמעט מוכנה.
arukhat ha'erev *kimat* *mukhana*
the dinner nearly ready

(86) Dissolve the tablet in water, don't chew it.

תמיס את הגלולה במים, אל תלעס אותה.
tamis *et* *haglula* *bema'im* *al* *tilas* *ota*
you will dissolve D.O. the tablet in water don't you will chew it

(87) Do monkeys actually like to eat bananas, or is that a myth?

קופים באמת אוהבים לאכול בננות, או שזה מיתוס?
kofim *be'emet* *ohavim* *le'ekhol* *bananot* *o* *sheze* *mitos*
monkeys actually they like to eat bananas or that this myth

(88) Do not believe everything you are told. It is often a lie.

אל תאמין לכל מה שאומרים לך. לעיתים קרובות.
al *ta'amin* *lekhol ma* *she'omrim* *lekha* *le'itim krovot*
don't you will believe to everything that they tell to you often

זה שקר.
ze *sheker*
this lie

(89) Do not cross the street while the light is red. That is dangerous.

אל תחצה את הרחוב באור אדום. זה מסוכן.
al *tekhatse* *et* *harekhov* *be'or* *adom* *ze* *mesukan*
don't you will cross D.O. the street at light red that dangerous

(90) Do vegetarians eat eggs?

צמחונים אוכלים ביצים?
tsimkhonim *okhlim* *beitsim*
vegetarians they eat eggs

(91) Do you believe in God?

את מאמינה באלוהים?
at *ma'amina* *be'elohim*
you you believe in God

(92) Do you have a cream for dry skin?

יש לך קרם לעור יבש?
yesh lakh *krem* *le'or* *yavesh*
you have cream for skin dry

(93) Do you have a driver's license yet?

יש לך כבר רישיון נהיגה?
yesh lakh *kvar* *rishayon* *nehiga*
you have yet license of driving

(94) Do you have a ladder I can borrow? I want to clean the windows.

יש לך סולם שאני יכול לשאול? אני רוצה לנקות את
yesh lekha *sulam* *she'ani* *yakhol* *lishol* *ani* *rotse* *lenakot* *et*
you have ladder that I I can to borrow I I want to clean D.O.

החלונות.
hakhalonot
the windows

9

Do you have a vase for the flowers?

(95) יש לך אגרטל בשביל הפרחים?
haprakhim bishvil agartal yesh lekha
the flowers for vase you have

Do you have all the ingredients necessary to make dinner?

(96) יש לך את כל המצרכים הדרושים על מנת להכין
lehakhin al menat hadrushim hamitsrakhim kol et yesh lekha
to make in order to the necessary the ingredients all D.O. you have

ארוחת ערב?
arukhat erev
dinner

Do you have an umbrella with you in case it rains?

(97) יש לך מטרייה איתך למקרה שירד גשם?
sheyered geshem lemikre itakh mitriya yesh lakh
that it rains in case with you umbrella you have

Do you have any book recommendations?

(98) יש לך ספרים שהיית ממליץ עליהם?
aleihem sheha'ita mamlits sfarim yesh lekha
about them that you would recommend books you have

Do you have coins for the machine? I only have bills.

(99) יש לך מטבעות בשביל המכונה? יש לי רק שטרות.
shtarot rak yesh li hamekhona bishvil matbe'ot yesh lakh
bills only I have the machine for coins you have

Do you have headaches frequently? If so, then you should not sit at the computer for so long.

(100) יש לך כאבי ראש לעיתים קרובות? אם כן, אז לא
lo az ken im le'itim krovot ke'evei rosh yesh lekha
not then yes if often headaches you have

כדאי שתשב מול המחשב לפרקי זמן ארוכים.
arukim zman lefirkei hamakhshev mul sheteshev kedai
long time for period of the computer facing that you will sit worthwhile

Do you have medicine for a cough?

(101) יש לך תרופה לשיעול?
leshi'ul trufa yesh lakh
for cough medicine you have

Do you have my new address?

(102) יש לכם את הכתובת החדשה שלי?
sheli hakhadasha haktovet et yesh lakhem
my the new the address D.O. you have

Do you hear the thunder? The storm is getting closer.

(103) את שומעת את הרעם? הסופה מתקרבת.
mitkarevet hasufa hara'am et shoma'at at
it comes close the storm the thunder D.O. you hear you

Do you know a good recipe for vegetable soup?

(104) אתה מכיר מתכון טוב למרק ירקות?
yerakot lemarak tov matkon makir ata
vegetables for soup of good recipe you know you

Do you know how to swim?

(105) אתן יודעות איך לשחות?
liskhot eikh yodot aten
to swim how you know you

Do you know the difference between vertical and horizontal?	אתה יודע מה ההבדל בין אנכי לאופקי? *ata yode'a ma hahevdel bein anakhi le'ofki* you know what the difference between vertical to horizontal	(106)
Do you mind if I stop by tomorrow afternoon?	אפשר לקפוץ אליך מחר אחרי הצוהריים? *efshar likpots eleikha makhar akharei hatsohora'im* possible to pop in to you tomorrow after the noon	(107)
Do you own your house or do you rent?	הבית בבעלותך או שאת שוכרת? *haba'it beva'alutekh o she'at sokheret* the house in your ownership or that you you rent	(108)
Do you play a musical instrument?	את מנגנת בכלי נגינה? *at menagenet bikhli negina* you you play with musical instrument	(109)
Do you promise not to tell anyone?	אתה מבטיח לא לגלות לאף אחד? *ata mavti'akh lo legalot le'af ekhad* you you promise not to reveal to nobody	(110)
Do you smoke? - No, never. I don't drink alcohol either.	אתה מעשן? - לא, אף פעם. אני גם לא שותה אלכוהול. *ata me'ashen lo af pa'am ani gam lo shote alkohol* you you smoke no never also I no I drink alcohol	(111)
Do you speak English? - A little.	את מדברת אנגלית? - קצת. *at medaberet anglit ktsat* you you speak English a little	(112)
Would you like sugar in your tea?	לשים סוכר בתה שלך? *lasim sukar bate shelakh* to put sugar in the tea your	(113)
Do you think that you will get the job? - Yes, I am quite optimistic.	את חושבת שתקבלי את המשרה? - כן, אני די *at khoshevet shetekabli et hamisra ken ani dei* you you think that you will get D.O. the position yes I quite אופטימית. *optimit* optimistic	(114)
Do you want a receipt?	אתה רוצה קבלה? *ata rotse kabala* you you want receipt	(115)
Do you want a ride home?	אתה רוצה טרמפ הביתה? *ata rotse tremp habaita* you want lift home	(116)
Does it bother you if I smoke?	יפריע לך אם אני אעשן? *yafri'a lekha im ani a'ashen* it will bother to you if I I will smoke	(117)

11

Does your family have a pet? - Yes, we have a dog.

(118) יש למשפחה שלכם חיית מחמד ? - כן, יש לנו כלב.

yesh lamishpakha	shelakhem	khayat makhmad	ken	yesh lanu	kelev
the family has	your	pet	yes	we have	dog

Doesn't everyone know that smoking is harmful to your health?

(119) האם לא כולם יודעים שהעישון פוגע בבריאות?

ha'im	lo	kulam	yodim	sheha'ishun	poge'a	babri'ut
is it that	not	everyone	they know	that the smoking	it harms	(for) the health

Don't go into the living room with wet shoes.

(120) אל תיכנסי לסלון עם נעליים רטובות.

al	tikansi	lasalon	im	na'ala'im	retuvot
don't	you will go	into the living room	with	shoes	wet

Don't tell me how the movie ends.

(121) אל תספר לי איך נגמר הסרט.

al	tesaper	li	eikh	nigmar	haseret
don't	you will tell	to me	how	it ends	the movie

Don't you have a sharper knife?

(122) אין לך סכין חדה יותר?

ein lekha	sakin	khada	yoter
don't you have	knife	sharp	more

Don't you want to take off your coat?

(123) אתה לא רוצה להוריד את המעיל שלך?

ata	lo	rotse	lehorid	et	hame'il	shelkha
you	no	you want	to take off	D.O.	the coat	your

Drive carefully. The roads are icy.

(124) סע בזהירות. הכבישים קפואים.

sa	bizhirut	hakvishim	kfu'im
drive	carefully	the roads	icy

Driving eight hours is too much. You should fly instead.

(125) לנסוע שמונה שעות זה יותר מידי. כדאי שתטוס במקום.

linso'a	shmone	sha'ot	ze	yoter midai	kedai shetatus	bimkom
to drive	eight	hours	this	too much	you should fly	instead

Due to fog, our plane could not land.

(126) המטוס שלנו לא היה יכול לנחות בגלל הערפל.

hamatos	shelanu	lo haya yakhol	linkhot	biglal	ha'arafel
the plane	our	it could not	to land	due to	the fog

Each country has its own unique culture.

(127) לכל מדינה יש את התרבות היחודית לה.

lekhol medina yesh	et	hatarbut	ha'ikhudit	la
each country has	D.O.	the culture	the unique	to it

Eight divided by two equals four.

(128) שמונה חלקי שתים שווה ארבע.

shmone	khelkei	shta'im	shave	arba
eight	divided by	two	equals	four

EU citizens can work anywhere in Europe.

(129) אזרחי האיחוד האירופאי יכולים לעבוד בכל אירופה.

ezrakhei	ha'ikhud	ha'eiropei	yekholim	la'avod	bekhol	eiropa
citizens of	the union	the European	they can	to work	in all of	Europe

(130) Everybody wants something different. We have to find a compromise.

כל אחד רוצה משהו שונה. אנחנו צריכים למצוא פשרה.

kol ekhad	rotse	mashehu	shone	anakhnu	tsrikhim	limtso	pshara
everyone	he wants	something	different	we	need to	to find	compromise

(131) Everyone is talking about climate change these days.

כולם מדברים על שינוי האקלים בימים אלה.

kulam	medabrim	al	shinui	ha'aklim	beyamim	ele
everyone	they talk	about	change of	the climate	in days	these

(132) Everyone stood on the platform and waved goodbye.

כולם עמדו על הרציף ונופפו לשלום.

kulam	amdu	al	haratsif	venofefu	leshalom
everyone	they stood	on	the platform	and they waved	to goodbye

(133) Everything together costs 2000 dollars including flights and hotels.

הכל יחד עולה 2000 דולר כולל טיסות ומלונות.

hakol	yakhad	ole	alpa'im	dolar	kolel	tisot	umelonot
everything	together	it costs	two thousand	dollar	including	flights	and hotels

(134) Excuse me for disturbing you, but there is a problem.

סליחה שאני מפריע לך, אבל יש בעיה.

slikha	she'ani	mafri'a	lakh	aval	yesh	be'aya
excuse me	that I	I disturb	to you	but	there is	problem

(135) Family is the most important thing.

משפחה זה הדבר החשוב ביותר.

mishpakha	ze	hadavar	hakhashuv	beyoter
family	this	the thing	the important	most

(136) Feeding the animals at the zoo is forbidden.

האכלת בעלי החיים בגן החיות אסורה.

ha'akhalat	ba'alei hakhayim	began hakhayot	asura
the feeding of	the animals	at the zoo	forbidden

(137) Finish your homework before watching television.

סיים את שיעורי הבית שלך לפני הצפייה בטלוויזיה.

sayem	et	shi'urei haba'it	shelkha	lifnei	hatsfiya	bateleviizya
finish	D.O.	the homework	your	before	the watching	(at) the television

(138) First highlight the lines, then copy and paste into a new document.

קודם סמן את השורות, ואז העתק והדבק אל מסמך חדש.

kodem	samen	et	hashurot	ve'az	ha'atek	vehadbek	el	mismakh	khadash
first	highlight	D.O.	the lines	and then	copy	and paste	into	document	new

(139) First put on your seatbelt and then start driving.

קודם חגור את חגורת הבטיחות ואז תתחיל לנהוג.

kodem	khagor	et	khagorat hebetikhut	ve'az	tatkhil	linhog
first	fasten	D.O.	the seatbelt	and then	you will start	to drive

(140) First put on your socks and then put on your shoes.

תנעל ואז שלך הגרביים את תגרוב קודם
tinal *ve'az* *shelkha* *hagarba'im* *et* *tigrov* *kodem*
you will put on / and then / your / the socks / D.O. / you will put on / first

את הנעליים.
hana'ala'im *et*
the shoes / D.O.

(141) First we're going food shopping, then we're barbecuing in the yard.

אנחנו ולאחר מכן לקנות אוכל, יוצאים אנחנו קודם
anakhnu *ule'akhar miken* *okhel* *liknot* *yotsim* *anakhnu* *kodem*
we / and then / food / to buy / we go out / we / first

עושים מנגל בחצר.
bakhatser *mangal* *osim*
in the yard / barbecue / we do

(142) For "marital status" you have to mark "single" since you're not married.

ב״מצב משפחתי״ עליך לסמן ״רווק״ מכיוון שאתה לא
lo *she'ata* *mikeivan* *ravak* *lesamen* *aleikha* *mishpakhti* *bematsav*
not / that you / since / single / to mark / on you / marital/family / for status

נשוי.
nasui
married

(143) For dessert there is chocolate ice cream.

לקינוח יש גלידת שוקולד.
shokolad *glidat* *yesh* *lekinu'akh*
chocolate / ice cream of / there is / for dessert

(144) For lunch there is chicken with rice.

לארוחת צהריים יש עוף עם אורז.
orez *im* *of* *yesh* *le'arukhat tsohora'im*
rice / with / of / there is / for lunch
(chicken)

(145) For me, not only is the price important, but also the quality.

בשבילי, לא רק המחיר חשוב, אלא גם האיכות.
ha'eikhut *gam* *ela* *khashuv* *hamekhir* *rak* *lo* *bishvili*
the quality / also / but / important / the price / only / not / for me

(146) For the assignment you can choose from these three topics.

אתה יכול לבחור מבין שלושת הנושאים האלה
ha'ele *hanosim* *shloshet* *mibein* *livkhor* *yakhol* *ata*
the these / the topics / three of / from among / to choose / you can / you

עבור התרגיל.
hatargil *avur*
the assignment / for

(147) For the last time, the answer is no.

בפעם האחרונה, התשובה היא לא.
lo *hi* *hatshuva* *ha'akhrona* *bapa'am*
no / it / the answer / the last / for the time

(148) From now on I will go to the gym regularly.

מעכשיו והלאה אני אלך לחדר הכושר באופן קבוע.
be'ofen kavu'a *lekhadar hakosher* *elekh* *ani* *va'hala* *me'akhshav*
on a regular basis / to the gym / I will go / I / and onward / from now

Garbage collection comes twice a week.

(149) **משאית הזבל מגיעה פעמיים בשבוע.**
masa'it *hazevel* *magi'a* *pa'ama'im* *beshavu'a*
truck of | the garbage | it comes | twice | per week

Gasoline prices are much higher than normal lately.

(150) **מחירי הדלק לאחרונה גבוהים בהרבה מהרגיל.**
mekhirei *hadelek* *la'akhrona* *gvohim* *beharbe* *meharagil*
prices of | the gas | lately | high | much more | than usual

Give me a minute to think about it.

(151) **תני לי דקה לחשוב על זה.**
tni *li* *daka* *lakhshov* *al* *ze*
give | to me | minute | to think | about | this

Give me all the details about your date.

(152) **ספרי לי הכל על הדייט שלך.**
sapri *li* *hakol* *al* *hadeit* *shelakh*
tell | to me | everything | about | the date | your

Green pants and yellow shoes? That looks funny.

(153) **מכנסיים ירוקים ונעליים צהובות? זה נראה מוזר.**
mikhnasa'im *yerukim* *vena'ala'im* *tsehubot* *ze* *nire* *muzar*
pants | green | and shoes | yellow | that | it looks | strange

Happy birthday!

(154) **יום הולדת שמח!**
yom *huledet* *same'akh*
day of | the birth | happy

Have a nice weekend. - Thanks, you too.

(155) **שיהיה לך סוף שבוע נעים. - תודה, גם לך.**
she'ihiye lakh *sof shavu'a* *na'im* *toda* *gam* *lakh*
that you will have | weekend | nice | thanks | also | to you

Have you already brushed your teeth?

(156) **צחצחת שיניים כבר?**
tsikhtsakhta *shina'im* *kvar*
you brushed | teeth | already

Have you already done your homework for school?

(157) **כבר הכנת את שיעורי הבית לבית הספר?**
kvar *hekhanta* *et* *shi'urei haba'it* *leveit hasefer*
already | you prepared | D.O. | the homework | for school

Have you already eaten?

(158) **אכלת כבר?**
akhalta *kvar*
you ate | already

Have you decided what you would like to order?

(159) **החלטתם מה תרצו להזמין?**
hekhlatetem *ma* *tirtsu* *lehazmin*
you decided | what | you will want | to order

Have you ever been to the Baltic Sea?

(160) **היית פעם בים הבלטי?**
ha'ita pa'am *bayam* *habalti*
were you ever | in the sea of | the Baltic

Have you, by any chance, seen my glasses? (161)

ראית במקרה את המשקפיים שלי?

ra'ita *bemikre* *et* *hamishkafa'im* *sheli*
you saw · by any chance · D.O. · the glasses · my

He copied my homework but somehow got a better grade than me. (162)

הוא העתיק ממני את שיעורי הבית שלי, אבל איכשהו

hu *he'etik* *mimeni* *et* *shi'urei haba'it* *sheli* *aval* *eikhshehu*
he · he copied · from me · D.O. · the homework · my · but · somehow

קיבל ציון גבוה יותר ממני.

kibel *tsiyun* *gavoha* *yoter* *mimeni*
he got · grade · high · more · than me

He got many gifts for his birthday. (163)

הוא קיבל הרבה מתנות ליום ההולדת שלו.

hu *kibel* *harbe* *matanot* *leyom* *hahuledet* *shelo*
he · he got · many · gifts · for day of · the birth · his

He has a cold and can not breathe through his nose. (164)

הוא מצונן ולא יכול לנשום מהאף.

hu *metsunan* *velo* *yakhol* *linshom* *meha'af*
he · he has a cold · and no · he can · to breathe · from the nose

He has been blind from birth. (165)

הוא עיוור מלידה.

hu *iver* *mileida*
he · blind · from birth

He has been in a coma for three weeks. (166)

הוא בתרדמת מזה שלושה שבועות.

hu *betardemet* *mize* *shlosha* *shavu'ot*
he · in coma · since · three · weeks

He hurt himself and had to go to the emergency room. (167)

הוא פצע את עצמו והיה צריך ללכת למיון.

hu *patsa* *et* *atsmo* *vehaya tsarikh* *lalekhet* *lemiyun*
he · he injured · D.O. · himself · and he had to · to go · to emergency room

He is an actor and also a great singer. (168)

הוא שחקן וגם זמר נהדר.

hu *sakhkan* *vegam* *zamar* *nehedar*
he · actor · and also · singer · great

He is an average student but an excellent athlete. (169)

הוא תלמיד ממוצע אבל אתלט מצוין.

hu *talmid* *memutsa* *aval* *atlet* *metsuyan*
he · student · average · but · athlete · excellent

He looks just like his father. (170)

הוא נראה בדיוק כמו אבא שלו.

hu *nire* *bediyuk* *kmo* *aba* *shelo*
he · he looks · exactly · like · father · his

He plays tennis quite well for a beginner. (171)

הוא משחק טניס די טוב בשביל מתחיל.

hu *mesakhek* *tenis* *dei* *tov* *bishvil* *matkhil*
he · he plays · tennis · quite · well · for · beginner

He ran a marathon and finished in first place. (172)

הוא רץ מרתון וסיים במקום הראשון.

hu *rats* *maraton* *vesiyem* *bamakom* *harishon*
he · he ran · marathon · and he finished · in the place · the first

He really deserves a vacation.

(173) מַמָּשׁ מַגִּיעָה לוֹ חוּפְשָׁה.

mamash	magi'a lo	khufsha
really	he deserves it	vacation

He refused my offer of help.

(174) הוּא סֵירֵב לְהַצָּעַת הָעֶזְרָה שֶׁלִּי.

hu	serev	lahatsa'at	ha'ezra	sheli
he	he refused	(to) offer of	the help	my

He suffers from a serious illness.

(175) הוּא סוֹבֵל מִמַּחֲלָה קָשָׁה.

hu	sovel	mimakhala	kasha
he	he suffers	from illness	serious

He thinks he is smarter than he really is.

(176) הוּא חוֹשֵׁב שֶׁהוּא חָכָם מִכְּפִי שֶׁהוּא בֶּאֱמֶת.

hu	khoshev	shehu	khakham	mikfi shehu	be'emet
he	he thinks	that he	smart	than he is	really

He told me that he is coming to the party but will be late.

(177) הוּא אָמַר לִי שֶׁיַּגִּיעַ לַמְּסִיבָּה אֲבָל שֶׁיְּאַחֵר.

hu	amar	li	sheyagi'a	lamsiba	aval	sheye'akher
he	he told	to me	that he will come	to the party	but	that he will be late

He tried very hard to cook something tasty.

(178) הוּא הִתְאַמֵּץ רַבּוֹת לְבַשֵּׁל מַשֶּׁהוּ טָעִים.

hu	hitamets	rabot	levashel	mashehu	ta'im
he	he made efforts	greatly	to cook	something	tasty

He will only accept the job if the company pays for his moving expenses.

(179) הוּא יַסְכִּים לְקַבֵּל אֶת הַמִּשְׂרָה רַק אִם הַחֶבְרָה

hu	yaskim	lekabel	et	hamisra	rak	im	hakhevra
he	he will agree	to accept	D.O.	the job	only	if	the company

תְּשַׁלֵּם אֶת הוֹצָאוֹת הַמַּעֲבָר שֶׁלּוֹ.

teshalem	et	hotsa'ot	hama'avar	shelo
it will pay	D.O.	expenses of	the moving	his

He works in medical research.

(180) הוּא עוֹבֵד בְּמֶחְקָר רְפוּאִי.

hu	oved	bemekhkar	refu'i
he	he works	in research	medical

He works well under pressure.

(181) הוּא עוֹבֵד טוֹב תַּחַת לַחַץ.

hu	oved	tov	takhat	lakhats
he	he works	well	under	pressure

Hello, how are you? - Good, thanks, and you?

(182) הַיי, מַה שְׁלוֹמֵךְ? - טוֹב, תּוֹדָה, וְאַתְּ?

hai	ma shlomekh	tov	toda	ve'at
hi	how are you	good	thanks	and you

Here are the keys to my apartment. Can you water my flowers while I'm gone?

(183) הִנֵּה הַמַּפְתְּחוֹת לַדִּירָה שֶׁלִּי. אַתָּה יָכוֹל לְהַשְׁקוֹת

hine	hamaftekhot	ladira	sheli	ata	yakhol	lehashkot
here	the keys	to the apartment	my	you	you can	to water

אֶת הַפְּרָחִים שֶׁלִּי כְּשֶׁאֲנִי לֹא נִמְצָא?

et	haprakhim	sheli	kshe'ani	lo nimtsa
D.O.	the flowers	my	when I	not present

17

(184) Here is my office number and also my cell phone number.

הנה המספר שלי במשרד, וגם מספר הנייד שלי.
hine hamispar sheli bamisrad, vegam mispar hanayad sheli
here the number my in my office and also number of the cell phone my

(185) Here is the book I was telling you about.

הנה הספר שסיפרתי לך עליו.
hine hasefer shesiparti lekha alav
here the book that I told to you about it

(186) Here is the list of ingredients needed for the cake.

הנה רשימת המצרכים שצריך לעוגה.
hine reshimat hamitsrakhim shetsarikh la'uga
here list of the ingredients that I need for the cake

(187) He's acting as though we never spoke about that.

הוא מתנהג כאילו מעולם לא דיברנו על זה.
hu mitnaheg ke'ilu me'olam lo dibarnu al ze
he he behaves as if never we spoke about this

(188) His dismissal from the company came as a surprise.

הפיטורים שלו מהחברה הגיעו בהפתעה.
hapiturim shelo mahakhevra higi'u behafta'a
the dismissal his from the company they arrived by surprise

(189) Hold my hand. We're crossing the street.

תחזיק לי את היד. אנחנו חוצים את הרחוב.
takhzik li et hayad. anakhnu khotsim et harekhov.
you will hold to me D.O. the hand we we cross D.O. the street

(190) Housing is becoming more and more expensive.

הדיור נהיה יותר ויותר יקר.
hadiyur nihiya yoter veyoter yakar
the housing it becomes more and more expensive

(191) How can I dispose of my old cell phone?

איך אני נפטר מהנייד הישן שלי?
eikh ani niftar mehanayad hayashan sheli
how I I dispose of the cell phone the old my

(192) How did you come up with this idea?

איך הגעת לרעיון הזה?
eikh higata lara'ayon haze
how you arrived to the idea the this

(193) How did you two meet?

איך נפגשתם?
eikh nifgashtem
how you met

(194) How do you play this game? Do you know the rules?

איך משחקים את המשחק הזה? אתה מכיר את הכללים?
eikh mesakhakim et hamiskhak haze? ata makir et haklalim?
how they play D.O. the game the this you you know D.O. the rules

(195) How do you spell that word?

איך מאייתים את המילה הזאת?
eikh me'aitim et hamila hazot
how they spell D.O. the word the this

How far is it to your friend's house? - It is very close, only ten minutes from here.

(196) כמה זה רחוק מהבית של חבר שלך? - זה קרוב

kama *ze* *rakhok* *mehaba'it* *shel* *khaver* *shelkha* *ze* *karov*

how much / this / far / from the house / of / friend / your / it / close

מאוד, רק עשר דקות מכאן.

me'od *rak* *eser* *dakot* *mikan*

very / only / ten / minutes / from here

How many cigarettes do you smoke a day? Anything more than zero is too many.

(197) כמה סיגריות אתה מעשן ביום? כל תשובה מעל

kama *sigaryot* *ata* *me'ashen* *beyom* *kol* *tshuva* *me'al*

how many / cigarettes / you / you smoke / in day / any / answer / above

אפס זה יותר מידי.

efes *ze* *yoter midai*

zero / this / too much

How many countries have you visited?

(198) בכמה מדינות היית?

bekhama *medinot* *ha'ita*

in how many / countries / you have been

How many letters are there in your language's alphabet?

(199) כמה אותיות יש באלפבית בשפה שלך?

kama *otiyot* *yesh* *ba'alefbet* *basafa* *shelkha*

how many / letters / there are / in the alphabet / in the language / your

How much money do I owe you?

(200) כמה כסף אני חייב לך?

kama *kesef* *ani* *khayav* *lekha*

how much / money / I / I owe / to you

How old is the boss? - I don't know, I guess around fifty.

(201) בת כמה הבוסית? - לא יודע, אני מעריך בסביבות

bat kama *habosit* *lo* *yode'a* *ani* *ma'arikh* *bisvivot*

how old / the boss / no / I know / I / I estimate / around

חמישים.

khamishim

fifty

I already called twice, but nobody answered.

(202) כבר התקשרתי פעמיים, אבל אף אחד לא ענה.

kvar *hitkasharti* *pa'ama'im* *aval* *af ekhad* *lo* *ana*

already / I called / twice / but / nobody / no / he answered

I already know several people in this city.

(203) אני כבר מכיר כמה אנשים בעיר הזאת.

ani *kvar* *makir* *kama* *anashim* *ba'ir* *hazot*

I / already / I know / several / people / in the city / the this

I always buy bread from the baker, not in the supermarket.

(204) אני תמיד קונה לחם מהאופה, לא בסופרמרקט.

ani *tamid* *kone* *lekhem* *meha'ofe* *lo* *basupermarket*

I / always / I buy / bread / from the baker / not / in the supermarket

I always have to read my children a story in the evening.

(205) אני תמיד חייב לקרוא לילדים שלי סיפור בערב.

ani *tamid* *khayav* *likro* *layeladim* *sheli* *sipur* *ba'erev*

I / always / I have to / to read / to the children / my / story / in the evening

I always take public transportation in the city.

(206) אני תמיד לוקח תחבורה ציבורית בתוך העיר.
ha'ir betokh tsiburit takhbura loke'akh tamid ani
the city in public transportation I take always I

I am always exhausted after running 10 km.

(207) אני תמיד מותש אחרי ריצה של עשרה ק״מ.
kilometer asara shel ritsa akharei mutash tamid ani
kilometer ten of running after exhausted always I

I am always very stressed out during exams.

(208) אני תמיד לחוץ מאוד במהלך בחינות.
bkhinot bemahalakh me'od lakhuts tamid ani
exams during very stressed out always I

I am happy with the location of the apartment.

(209) אני מרוצה מהמיקום של הדירה.
hadira shel mehamikum merutse ani
the apartment of from the location satisfied I

I am in a hurry. I'm late.

(210) אני ממהר. אני מאחר.
me'akher ani memaher ani
I am late I I hurry I

I am interested in other countries and cultures.

(211) אני מתעניין במדינות ותרבויות אחרות.
akherot vetarbuyot bimdinot mitanyen ani
other and cultures in countries I am interested I

I am lucky that all my grandchildren live nearby.

(212) אני בר מזל שכל נכדיי גרים בסביבה.
basviva garim nekhadai shekol bar mazal ani
nearby they live my grandchildren that all lucky I

I am new to the building. I don't know any neighbors yet.

(213) אני חדש בבניין. אני לא מכיר את השכנים עדיין.
ada'in hashkhenim et makir lo ani babinyan khadash ani
yet the neighbors D.O. I know no I in the building new I

I am not hungry right now. I don't want to eat anything.

(214) אני לא רעב כרגע. אני לא רוצה לאכול כלום.
klum le'ekhol rotse lo ani karega ra'ev lo ani
nothing to eat I want no I right now hungry not I

I am not interested in politics.

(215) אני לא מתעניין בפוליטיקה.
bepolitika mitanyen lo ani
in politics I am interested no I

I am proud of you. You did a great job.

(216) אני גאה בך. עשית עבודה נהדרת.
nehederet avoda asita bekha ge'a ani
great job you did of you proud I

I am quite surprised that the apartment is so cheap. I wonder what's wrong with it.

(217) אני די מופתע שהדירה כל כך זולה. אני תוהה
tohe ani zola kol kakh shehadira mufta dei ani
I wonder I cheap so that the apartment surprised quite I

מה לא בסדר איתה.
ita beseder lo ma
with it okay not what

I am the youngest in our family.

(218) אני הצעיר ביותר במשפחה שלנו.
shelanu bamishpakha beyoter hatsa'ir ani
our in the family most the young I

I bought a digital watch. It runs more accurately than my old wind-up watch.

(219) קניתי שעון דיגיטלי. הוא עובד בצורה מדויקת יותר
yoter meduyeket betsura oved hu digitali sha'on kaniti
more accurate in a way it works it digital watch I bought

בהשוואה לשעון הקפיצים המכאני הישן שלי.
sheli hayashan hamekhani hakfitsim lisha'on behashva'a
my the old the mechanical the springs to watch in comparison

I bought a used car, not a new one.

(220) קניתי מכונית משומשת, לא חדשה.
khadasha lo meshumeshet mekhonit kaniti
new not used car I bought

I bought too many oranges, and I have no idea what to do with them.

(221) קניתי יותר מידי תפוזים ואין לי מושג מה לעשות
la'asot ma musag ve'ein li tapuzim yoter midai kaniti
to do what idea and I don't have oranges too many I bought

איתם.
itam
with them

I bought myself a bigger computer monitor. It's better for my eyes.

(222) קניתי לעצמי מסך מחשב גדול יותר. זה טוב יותר
yoter tov ze yoter gadol makhshev masakh le'atsmi kaniti
more good this more big computer monitor of for myself I bought

לעיניים שלי.
sheli la'eina'im
my for the eyes

I bought myself a dark blue suit.

(223) קניתי לעצמי חליפה בצבע כחול כהה.
kehe kakhol betseva khalifa le'atsmi kaniti
dark blue of color suit for myself I bought

I bought these sunglasses in Europe.

(224) קניתי את משקפי השמש האלה באירופה.
be'eiropa ha'ele mishkefei hashemesh et kaniti
in Europe the these the sunglasses D.O. I bought

I can barely move without pain.

(225) אני בקושי יכול לזוז בלי שיכאב לי.
li she'ikhav bli lazuz yakhol bekoshi ani
to me that it will hurt without to move I can barely I

I can not decide that myself because I have to ask the boss first.

(226) אני לא יכול להחליט על כך בעצמי כי אני צריך
tsarikh ani ki be'atsmi al kakh lehakhlit yakhol lo ani
I need to I because myself about it to decide I can no I

לשאול את הבוס קודם.
kodem habos et lishol
first the boss D.O. to ask

(227) I speak English, French, and Persian quite well.

אני מדבר אנגלית, צרפתית, ופרסית די טוב.
ani medaber anglit tsarfatit uparsit dei tov
I — I speak — English — French — and Persian — quite — well

(228) I can't answer my phone right now, so please leave a message.

אני לא יכול לענות לטלפון שלי כרגע, אז בבקשה
ani lo yakhol la'anot latelefon sheli karega az bevakasha
I — no — I can — to answer — to the telephone — my — right now — so — please

השאירו הודעה.
hashiru hoda'a
leave — message

(229) I can't eat any more. I'm stuffed!

אני לא יכול לאכול עוד. אני מפוצץ !
ani lo yakhol le'ekhol od ani mefutsats
I — no — I can — to eat — more — I — I am bursting

(230) I can't explain how the chocolate disappeared.

אני לא יודע להסביר איך השוקולד נעלם.
ani lo yode'a lehasbir eikh hashokolad ne'elam
I — no — I know — to explain — how — the chocolate — it disappeared

(231) I can't find my keys anywhere.

אני לא מוצא את המפתחות שלי באף מקום.
ani lo motse et hamaftekhot sheli be'af makom
I — no — I find — D.O. — the keys — my — in any place

(232) I can't hear so well anymore.

אני לא שומע טוב כמו פעם.
ani lo shome'a tov kmo pa'am
I — no — I hear — well — like — once

(233) I can't help you right now. I'm in the middle of cooking dinner.

אני לא יכול לעזור לך כרגע. אני באמצע
ani lo yakhol la'azor lakh karega ani be'emtsa
I — no — I can — to help — to you — right now — I — in the middle of

הבישולים של ארוחת הערב.
habishulim shel arukhat ha'erev
the cooking — of — the dinner

(234) I can't read your handwriting.

אני לא מסוגל לקרוא את כתב היד שלך.
ani lo mesugal likro et ktav hayad shelakh
I — no — I am able — to read — D.O. — the handwriting — your

(235) I can't run because of pain in one of my toes.

אני לא יכול לרוץ בגלל כאב באחת הבהונות.
ani lo yakhol laruts biglal ke'ev be'akhat habehonot
I — no — I can — to run — because of — pain — in one of — the toes

(236) I can't understand anything when you all speak at the same time.

אני לא יכול להבין כלום כשאתם מדברים כולכם
ani lo yakhol lehavin klum kshe'atem medabrim kulkhem
I — no — I can — to understand — nothing — when you — you speak — all of you

בבת אחת.
bevat akhat
at the same time

I can't wait to see you again.

(237) אני כבר לא יכול לחכות לראות אתכם שוב.
shuv etkhem lirot lekhakot yakhol lo kvar ani
again you to see to wait I can no already I

I catch a cold at least once every winter.

(238) אני מתקרר לפחות פעם אחת כל חורף.
khoref kol pa'am akhat lefakhot mitkarer ani
winter every once at least I catch a cold I

I changed my opinion after getting new information.

(239) שיניתי את דעתי אחרי שקיבלתי מידע חדש.
khadash meida shekibalti akharei da'ati et shiniti
new information that I got after my opinion D.O. I changed

I checked the bill. Everything is correct.

(240) בדקתי את החשבון. הכל נכון.
nakhon hakol hakheshbon et badakti
correct everything the bill D.O. I checked

I completely forgot about the appointment.

(241) לגמרי שכחתי מהתור.
mehator shakhakhti legamrei
of the appointment I forgot completely

I cooked a special meal for you.

(242) בישלתי ארוחה מיוחדת בשבילך.
bishvilkha meyukhedet arukha bishalti
for you special meal I cooked

I couldn't see anything because of all the dirt on the window.

(243) לא יכולתי לראות כלום בגלל כל הלכלוך על החלון.
hakhalon al halikhlukh kol biglal klum lirot yakholti lo
the window on the dirt all because of nothing to see I could no

I did not have to pay anything. The repair was covered by the warranty.

(244) לא הייתי צריך לשלם כלום. התיקון כוסה על ידי
al yedei kusa hatikun klum leshalem ha'iti tsarikh lo
by it was covered the repair nothing to pay I had to no

האחריות.
ha'akhrayut
the warranty

I did not realize it was already so late. I have to go.

(245) לא שמתי לב שכל כך מאוחר. אני צריך ללכת.
lalekhet tsarikh ani me'ukhar shekol kakh samti lev lo
to go I need I late that so I paid attention no

I didn't understand your question. Please repeat it.

(246) לא הבנתי את השאלה שלך. חזור עליה בבקשה.
bevakasha khazor aleiha shelkha hashe'ela et hevanti lo
please repeat it your the question D.O. I understood no

I do not know if we have this shoe in your size. I'll check the stock room.

(247) אני לא יודע אם יש לנו את הנעל הזאת במידה שלך.
shelkha bamida hazot hana'al et yesh lanu im yode'a lo ani
your in the size the this the shoe D.O. we have if I know no I

אני אבדוק במחסן.
bamakhsan evdok ani
in the storeroom I will check I

(248) I don't like baths, I prefer showers.

אני לא אוהב אמבטיות, אני מעדיף דוש.
dush — ma'adif — ani — ambatyot — ohev — lo — ani
shower — I prefer — I — baths — I like — no — I

(249) I don't allow my kids to watch TV for more than thirty minutes per day.

אני לא מרשה לילדים שלי לצפות בטלוויזיה יותר
yoter — batelevizya — litspot — sheli — layeladim — marshe — lo — ani
more — at television — to watch — my — to the kids — I allow — no — I

משלושים דקות ביום.
beyom — dakot — mishloshim
per day — minutes — than thirty

(250) I don't doubt that you're right, but you still have to convince everyone else.

אני לא מטיל ספק בזה שאתה צודק, אבל אתה עדיין
ada'in — ata — aval — tsodek — she'ata — beze — safek — metil — lo — ani
still — you — but — right — that you — of this — doubt — I cast — no — I

צריך לשכנע את כל האחרים.
ha'akherim — kol — et — leshakhne'a — tsarikh
the others — all — D.O. — to convince — you need to

(251) I don't earn enough money to afford a new car.

אני לא מרוויח מספיק כסף כדי להרשות לעצמי
le'atsmi — leharshot — kedei — kesef — maspik — marvi'akh — lo — ani
for myself — to allow — in order to — money — enough — I earn — no — I

רכב חדש.
khadash — rekhev
new — car

(252) I don't feel well. I think I have a fever.

אני לא חש בטוב. נראה לי שיש לי חום.
khom — sheyesh li — li — nire — khash betov — lo — ani
fever — that I have — to me — it seems — I feel well — no — I

(253) I don't have a landline, but I have a cell phone.

אין לי טלפון קווי, אבל יש לי נייד.
nayad — yesh li — aval — kavi — telefon — ein li
cell phone — I have — but — line — telephone — I don't have

(254) I don't have an apartment yet. I'm living with a friend for the time being.

אין לי דירה עדיין. אני גר אצל חברה בינתיים.
beinta'im — khavera — etsel — gar — ani — ada'in — dira — ein li
in the meantime — friend — at — I live — I — yet — apartment — I don't have

(255) I don't have kids yet, but I hope to eventually have three.

אין לי ילדים עדיין, אבל אני מקווה שבסופו של דבר
shebesofo shel davar — mekave — ani — aval — ada'in — yeladim — ein li
in the end — I hope — I — but — yet — kids — I don't have

יהיו לי שלושה.
shlosha — ihiyu li
three — I will have

I don't know that word. I should look it up in the dictionary.

אני לא מכיר את המילה הזאת. כדאי לי לחפש (256)
ani lo makir et hamila hazot kedai li lekhapes
I no I know D.O. the word the that worthwhile for me to look up

אותה במילון.
ota bamilon
it in the dictionary

I don't mind if you take the car today.

לא אכפת לי אם תיקח את האוטו היום. (257)
lo ikhpat li im tikakh et ha'oto hayom
I don't mind if you will take D.O. the car today

I don't ride my motorcycle when it is cold.

אני לא רוכב על האופנוע שלי כשקר. (258)
ani lo rokhev al ha'ofano'a sheli kshekar
I no I ride on the motorcycle my when cold

I don't think you'll get that much money for the car. That is not realistic.

אני לא חושב שתקבל כל כך הרבה כסף על (259)
ani lo khoshev shetekabel kol kakh harbe kesef al
I no I think that you will get so much money for

המכונית. זה לא מציאותי.
hamekhonit ze lo metsi'uti
the car that not realistic

I don't understand the humor of this comedian.

אני לא מבין את ההומור של הקומיקאי הזה. (260)
ani lo mevin et hahumor shel hakomikai haze
I no I understand D.O. the humor of the comedian the this

I don't understand what I can't explain.

אני לא מבין מה שאני לא מסוגל להסביר. (261)
ani lo mevin ma she'ani lo mesugal lehasbir
I no I understand what that I no I am able to explain

I don't understand what you're saying. Can you please say it again more simply?

אני לא מבין מה אתה אומר. אתה יכול בבקשה (262)
ani lo mevin ma ata omer ata yakhol bevakasha
I no I understand what you you say you you can please

לומר זאת שוב בצורה פשוטה יותר?
lomar zot shuv betsura pshuta yoter
to say this again in manner simple more

I don't want a job that makes me work on the weekend.

אני לא רוצה עבודה שמחייבת אותי לעבוד (263)
ani lo rotse avoda shemekhayevet oti la'avod
I no I want job that (it) makes me to work

בסוף השבוע.
besof hashavu'a
on the weekend

I eat an apple every day with my breakfast.

אני אוכל תפוח כל יום עם ארוחת הבוקר. (264)
ani okhel tapu'akh kol yom im arukhat haboker
I I eat apple every day with meal of the morning

25

I exercise a lot and eat a lot of vegetables.

אני מתאמן המון ואוכל הרבה ירקות. (265)

yerakot harbe ve'okhel hamon mitamen ani
vegetables a lot and I eat a lot I exercise I

I find this chair to be very un-comfortable.

הכיסא הזה מאוד לא נוח לי. (266)

li no'akh lo me'od haze hakise
to me comfortable not very the this the chair

I forgot my passport, so I had to quickly go back home to get it.

שכחתי את הדרכון שלי, אז הייתי צריך לחזור הביתה (267)

habaita lakhzor ha'iti tsarikh az sheli hadarkon et shakhakhti
home to return I had to so my the passport D.O. I forgot

מהר כדי להביא אותו.

oto lehavi kedei maher
it to obtain in order to quickly

I forgot your birthday. I have quite a guilty conscience.

שכחתי את יום ההולדת שלך. יש לי נקיפות מצפון. (268)

matspun nekifot yesh li shelakh yom hahuledet et shakhakhti
conscience pangs of I have your the birthday D.O. I forgot

I get along well with my daughter-in-law.

אני מסתדר טוב עם כלתי. (269)

kalati im tov mistader ani
my daughter-in-law with well I get along I

I get up every morning at six.

אני קם כל בוקר בשש. (270)

beshesh boker kol kam ani
at six morning every I wake up I

I go grocery shopping once a week.

אני עושה קניות פעם בשבוע. (271)

beshavu'a pa'am kniyot ose ani
per week once shopping I do I

I got married very young.

התחתנתי מאוד צעיר. (272)

tsa'ir me'od hitkhatanti
young very I got married

I got the visa from the embassy.

קיבלתי את האשרה מהשגרירות. (273)

mehashagrirut ha'ashra et kibalti
from the embassy the visa D.O. I got

I brought you a gift. It's on the table.

הבאתי לך מתנה. היא על השולחן. (274)

hashulkhan al hi matana lekha heveti
the table on it gift for you I brought

I had an accident with the car. Now I have to report the damage to the insurance company.

עשיתי תאונה עם האוטו. עכשיו אני צריך לדווח על (275)

al ledave'akh tsarikh ani akhshav ha'oto im te'una asiti
on to report I need I now the car with accident I did

הנזק לחברת הביטוח.

habitu'akh lekhevrat hanezek
the insurance to company of the damage

I had great difficulty finding a parking space.

היה לי מאוד קשה למצוא מקום חניה. (276)
khanaya mekom limtso kashe me'od li haya
parking space of to find difficult very for me it was

I had to wait a long time for an answer. But I got the job in the end.

הייתי צריך להמתין זמן ארוך לתשובה. אבל קיבלתי (277)
kibalti aval litshuva arokh zman lehamtin ha'iti tsarikh
I got but for answer long time to wait I had to

את המשרה בסוף.
basof hamisra et
in the end the position D.O.

I hate how my voice sounds.

אני שונא איך שהקול שלי נשמע. (278)
nishma sheli shehakol eikh sone ani
it sounds my that the voice how I hate I

I have a cavity in my tooth. I have to go to the dentist.

יש לי חור בשן. אני צריך ללכת לרופא השיניים. (279)
lerofe hashina'im lalekhet tsarikh ani bashen khor yesh li
to the dentist to go I need I in the tooth cavity I have

I have a cold. I can't smell anything.

אני מצונן. אני לא מריח כלום. (280)
klum meri'akh lo ani metsunan ani
nothing I smell no I I have a cold I

I have a difficult week ahead of me. I have to work overtime every day.

מחכה לי שבוע קשה. אני צריך לעבוד שעות נוספות (281)
nosafot sha'ot la'avod tsarikh ani kashe shavu'a li mekhake
additional hours to work I need I hard week for me it awaits

כל יום.
yom kol
day every

I have a good relationship with my parents.

יש לי יחסים טובים עם ההורים שלי. (282)
sheli hahorim im tovim yekhasim yesh li
my the parents with good relations I have

I have a lot to do at the moment. - Then I don't want to disturb you any longer.

יש לי הרבה דברים לעשות כרגע. - אז אני לא (283)
lo ani az karega la'asot dvarim harbe yesh li
no I then at the moment to do things many I have

רוצה להפריע לך יותר.
yoter lekha lehafri'a rotse
more to you to disturb I want

I have a small child and can't work eight hours a day. Therefore I would like to work half-days.

יש לי ילדה קטנה ואני לא יכול לעבוד שמונה שעות (284)
sha'ot shmone la'avod yakhol lo va'ani ktana yalda yesh li
hours eight to work I can no and I small child I have

ביום. לכן אני מעוניין לעבוד חצאי ימים.
yamim khatsa'ei la'avod me'unyan ani lakhen beyom
days half of to work I am interested I therefore per day

I have changed my mind. I am coming with you.

שיניתי את דעתי. אני בא איתך. (285)
itkha ba ani da'ati et shiniti
with you I come I my mind D.O. I changed

I have injured myself. My hand is bleeding.

פצעתי את עצמי. היד שלי מדממת. (286)
medamemet sheli hayad atsmi et patsati
it bleeds my the hand myself D.O. I injured

I have many nice memories from my childhood.

יש לי זכרונות רבים נעימים מהילדות שלי. (287)
sheli mehayaldut ne'imim rabim zikhronot yesh li
my from the childhood nice many memories I have

I have no energy left for exercise in the evening.

לא נשאר לי כוח להתאמן בערב. (288)
ba'erev lehitamen ko'akh li nishar lo
in the evening to exercise energy to me it remains no

I have ten years of experience in this field.

יש לי עשר שנות ניסיון בתחום הזה. (289)
haze batkhum nisayon shnot eser yesh li
the this in the field experience years of ten I have

I have three kids and have no time anymore for my hobbies.

יש לי שלושה ילדים ואין לי זמן בכלל יותר (290)
yoter bikhlal zman ve'ein li yeladim shlosha yesh li
anymore at all time and I don't have kids three I have

לתחביבים שלי.
sheli latakhbivim
my for the hobbies

I have to charge my phone. The battery is empty.

אני צריך לטעון את הפלאפון שלי. הסוללה ריקה. (291)
reika hasolela sheli hapelefon et liton tsarikh ani
empty the battery my the cell phone D.O. to charge I need I

I have two copies of the book. Do you want one?

יש לי שני עותקים של הספר. אתה רוצה אחד? (292)
ekhad rotse ata hasefer shel otakim shnei yesh li
one you want you the book of copies two of I have

I haven't been able to move my arm since the operation.

אני לא יכול להזיז את הזרוע שלי מאז הניתוח. (293)
hanitu'akh me'az sheli hazro'a et lehaziz yakhol lo ani
the operation since my the arm D.O. to move I can no I

I haven't eaten anything all day, so I'm quite hungry.

לא אכלתי כלום כל היום, לכן אני די רעב. (294)
ra'ev dei ani lakhen hayom kol klum akhalti lo
hungry quite I so the day all nothing I ate no

I haven't seen you in ages, but you haven't changed at all.

לא ראיתי אותך שנים, אבל לא השתנית בכלל. (295)
bikhlal hishtaneit lo aval shanim otakh ra'iti lo
at all you changed no but years you I saw no

I hit a big tree with my car. The tree is fine, but my car was destroyed.

(296) פגעתי בעץ גדול עם האוטו. העץ בסדר, אבל האוטו
| pagati | be'ets | gadol | im | ha'oto | ha'ets | beseder | aval | ha'oto |
| I hit | at tree | big | with | the car | the tree | fine | but | the car |

נהרס.
neheras
it was destroyed

I hope you haven't been waiting long.

(297) אני מקווה שאתה לא מחכה המון זמן.
| ani | mekave | she'ata | lo | mekhake | hamon | zman |
| I | I hope | that you | no | you wait | a lot | time |

I immediately recognized my mother by her voice.

(298) מיד זיהיתי את אמא שלי דרך הקול שלה.
| miyad | zihiti | et | ima | sheli | derekh | hakol | shela |
| immediately | I recognized | D.O. | mother | my | by means of | the voice | her |

I injured my knee. Now I can't run.

(299) פצעתי את הברך שלי. עכשיו אני לא יכול לרוץ.
| patsati | et | haberekh | sheli | akhshav | ani | lo | yakhol | laruts |
| I injured | D.O. | the knee | my | now | I | no | I can | to run |

I just need to quickly get some cash from the ATM.

(300) אני רק צריך להוציא קצת כסף זריז מהכספומט.
| ani | rak | tsarikh | lehotsi | ksat | kesef | zariz | mehakaspomat |
| I | just | I need | to take out | a little | money | quickly | from the ATM |

I know a bit about dinosaurs, but I'm not an expert.

(301) אני יודע קצת על דינוזאורים, אבל אני לא מומחה.
| ani | yode'a | ktsat | al | dinoza'urim | aval | ani | lo | mumkhe |
| I | I know | a bit | about | dinosaurs | but | I | not | expert |

I learned so much before the exam. Afterwards I forgot almost everything.

(302) למדתי כל כך הרבה לפני הבחינה. אחריה שכחתי כמעט
| lamadeti | kol kakh | harbe | lifnei | habkhina | akhareiha | shakhakhti | kimat |
| I learned | so | much | before | the exam | after it | I forgot | almost |

הכל.
hakol
everything

I forgot my luggage in a locker at the train station.

(303) שכחתי את הכבודה שלי בתא אחסון בתחנת הרכבת.
| shakhakhti | et | hakvuda | sheli | beta | ikhsun | betakhanat | harakevet |
| I forgot | D.O. | the luggage | my | in cell of | storage | in station of | the train |

I like listening to folk music on the radio.

(304) אני אוהב להאזין למוזיקה אתנית ברדיו.
| ani | ohev | leha'azin | lemuzika | etnit | baradyo |
| I | I like | to listen | to music | folk | on the radio |

I like playing tennis, squash, and any other racquet sport.

(305) אני אוהב לשחק טניס, סקווש, וכל משחק מחבט
| ani | ohev | lesakhek | tenis | skwosh | vekhol | miskhak | makhbet |
| I | I like | to play | tennis | squash | and any | game of | racquet |

אחר.
akher
other

(306) I like to eat bread with honey and butter for breakfast.

אני אוהב לאכול לחם עם דבש וחמאה לארוחת בוקר.

ani	ohev	le'ekhol	lekhem	im	dvash	vekhema	le'arukhat	boker
I	I like	to eat	bread	with	honey	and butter	for meal of	morning

(307) I like to listen to music on the radio while I'm driving.

אני אוהב להאזין למוזיקה ברדיו כשאני נוהג.

ani	ohev	leha'azin	lemuzika	baradyo	kshe'ani	noheg
I	I like	to listen	to music	on the radio	while I	I drive

(308) I lost fifteen percent of my body weight over the last year.

הורדתי חמישה עשר אחוז ממשקל הגוף שלי בשנה

horadeti	khamisha asar	akhuz	mimishkal haguf	sheli	bashana
I reduced)	fifteen	percent	of the body weight	my	in the year

האחרונה.

ha'akhrona
the last

(309) I lost my shoes when my feet sank into the mud.

איבדתי את הנעליים שלי כשכפות הרגליים שלי שקעו

ibadeti	et	hana'ala'im	sheli	kshekapot haragla'im	sheli	shaku
I lost	D.O.	the shoes	my	when the feet	my	they sank

בבוץ.

babots
into the mud

(310) I lost my wedding ring while swimming in the lake.

איבדתי את טבעת הנישואין שלי כששחיתי באגם.

ibadeti	et	taba'at	hanisu'in	sheli	kshesakhiti	ba'agam
I lost	D.O.	ring of	the marriage	my	as I swam	in the lake

(311) I love my family even though they drive me crazy most of the time.

אני אוהב את המשפחה שלי למרות שהיא משגעת

ani	ohev	et	hamishpakha	sheli	lamrot	shehi	meshaga'at
I	I love	D.O.	the family	my	even though	that it	it makes crazy

אותי רוב הזמן.

oti	rov hazman
me	most of the time

(312) I measured the room. It is exactly 20 m².

מדדתי את החדר. הוא בדיוק 20 מ"ר.

madadeti	et	hakheder	hu	bediyuk	esrim	meter meruba
I measured	D.O.	the room	it	exactly	twenty	square meters

(313) I missed the train, but another one is coming in twenty minutes.

פספסתי את הרכבת, אבל רכבת נוספת מגיעה עוד

fisfasti	et	harakevet	aval	rakevet	nosefet	magi'a	od
I missed	D.O.	the train	but	train	additional	it arrives	another

עשרים דקות.

esrim	dakot
twenty	minutes

(314) I need some good hand cream because my hands are so dry.

אני צריך קרם ידיים טוב כי הידיים שלי כל כך יבשות.
ani tsarikh krem yada'im tov ki hayada'im sheli kol kakh yeveshot
I · I need · cream of · hands · good · because · the hands · my · so · dry

(315) I need to pick up my daughter from school no later than three o'clock.

אני צריך לאסוף את הבת שלי מבית הספר לא מאוחר יותר משעה שלוש.
ani tsarikh le'esof et habat sheli mibeit hasefer lo me'ukhar yoter misha'a shalosh
I · I need · to pick up · D.O. · the daughter · my · from the school · no · late · more · than hour of · three

(316) I need to take the car into the shop to get fixed.

אני צריך לקחת את המכונית למוסך לתיקונים.
ani tsarikh lakakhat et hamekhonit lamusakh letikunim
I · I need · to take · D.O. · the car · to the garage · for repairs

(317) I only buy organic fruit and vegetables.

אני קונה רק פירות וירקות אורגניים.
ani kone rak peirot viyrakot organi'im
I · I buy · only · fruits · and vegetables · organic

(318) I only just arrived. Do you mind if I use the toilet before we start chatting?

בדיוק הגעתי. אכפת לך שאני אלך לשירותים לפני שנתחיל את השיחה?
bediyuk higati. ikhpat lekha she'ani elekh lasherutim lifnei shenatkhil et hasikha?
exactly · I arrived · do you mind · that I · I will go · to the restroom · before · that we will start · D.O. · the conversation

(319) I plan to retire at the end of the year.

אני מתכננת לפרוש בסוף השנה.
ani metakhnenet lifrosh besof hashana
I · I plan · to retire · at end of · the year

(320) I put only butter on my bread.

אני שם רק חמאה על הלחם שלי.
ani sam rak khema al halekhem sheli
I · I put · only · butter · on · the bread · my

(321) I ran as fast as I could, but I was still late for the bus.

רצתי הכי מהר שיכולתי, אבל עדיין איחרתי את האוטובוס.
ratsti hakhi maher sheyakholti, aval ada'in ekharti et ha'otobus
I ran · the most · fast · that I could · but · still · I was late for · D.O. · the bus

(322) I rang the doorbell, but nobody was at home.

צלצלתי בפעמון, אבל אף אחד לא היה בבית.
tsiltsalti bapa'amon, aval af ekhad lo haya baba'it
I rang · at the doorbell · but · nobody · no · he was · at home

(323) I really enjoy this job, despite the low pay.

אני באמת מאוד נהנה מהעבודה הזאת, למרות השכר
ani be'emet me'od nehene meha'avoda hazot lamrot hasakhar
I really very much I enjoy of the job the this despite the pay

הנמוך.
hanamukh
the low

(324) I really like Japanese cuisine.

אני מאוד אוהב את המטבח היפני.
ani me'od ohev et hamitbakh hayapani
I very much I like D.O. the cuisine the Japanese

(325) I searched everywhere, but I can't find my sunglasses.

חיפשתי בכל מקום, אבל אני לא מוצא את
khipasti bekhol makom aval ani lo motse et
I searched in every place but I no I find D.O.

משקפי השמש שלי.
mishkefei hashemesh sheli
the sunglasses my

(326) I should clean up before the guests arrive.

כדאי שאני אנקה לפני שהאורחים יגיעו.
kedai she'ani anake lifnei sheha'orkhim yagi'u
worthwhile that I I will clean up before that the guests they will arrive

(327) I slipped because the floor is slippery.

החלקתי בגלל שהרצפה מחליקה.
hekhlakti biglal sheharitspa makhlika
I slipped because that the floor slippery

(328) I sold our old car and bought a new one.

מכרתי את המכונית הישנה שלנו וקניתי אחת חדשה.
makharti et hamekhonit hayeshana shelanu vekaniti akhat khadasha
I sold D.O. the car the old our and I bought one new

(329) I still have to pack my suitcase for the trip.

אני צריך עדיין לארוז את המזוודה שלי לפני הנסיעה.
ani tsarikh ada'in le'eroz et hamizvada sheli lifnei hanesi'a
I I need still to pack D.O. the suitcase my before the trip

(330) I still live with my parents.

אני עדיין גר עם ההורים.
ani ada'in gar im hahorim
I still I live with the parents

(331) I talk to my mother every day.

אני מדבר עם אמא שלי כל יום.
ani medaber im ima sheli kol yom
I I talk with mother my every day

(332) I think about many things differently now than before I had children.

אני חושב על הרבה דברים באופן שונה עכשיו
ani khoshev al harbe dvarim be'ofen shone akhshav
I I think about many things in manner different now

בהשוואה לתקופה שלפני שהיו לי ילדים.
behashva'a latkufa shelifnei shehayu li yeladim
in comparison to the period that before that I had children

(333) I think he is telling the truth, but I'm not completely sure.

אני חושב שהוא אומר את האמת, אבל אני לא לגמרי
ani khoshev shehu omer et ha'emet aval ani lo legamrei
I think that he he tells D.O. the truth but I not completely

בטוח.
batu'akh
sure

(334) I think I made a good impression at the job interview.

אני חושבת שעשיתי רושם טוב בראיון העבודה.
ani khoshevet she'asiti roshem tov bere'ayon ha'avoda
I think that I made impression good at interview of the job

(335) I think the movie was good. What do you think?

אני חושבת שהסרט היה טוב. מה את חושבת?
ani khoshevet shehaseret haya tov ma at khoshevet
I think that the movie it was good what you you think

(336) I thought that we could drive together and split the cost of gas.

חשבתי שנוכל לנסוע ביחד ולחלוק את הוצאות
khashavti shenukhal linso'a beyakhad velakhlok et hotsa'ot
I thought that we will be able to drive together and to split D.O. costs of

הדלק.
hadelek
the gas

(337) I understand you better when you don't speak in dialect.

אני מבין אותך יותר טוב כשאתה לא מדבר בניב
ani mevin otkha yoter tov kshe'ata lo medaber beniv
I I understand you more good when you no you speak in dialect

אחר.
akher
another

(338) I used to babysit him when he was a baby.

הייתי שומר עליו כשהיה תינוק.
ha'iti shomer alav kshehaya tinok
I used to guard (on) him when he was baby

(339) I used to be unemployed, but I recently got a job.

הייתי מובטל, אבל לאחרונה השגתי עבודה.
ha'iti muvtal aval la'akhrona hisagti avoda
I used to be unemployed but recently I obtained job

(340) I used to live in the city, but now I live in the suburbs with my family.

הייתי גר בעיר, אבל עכשיו אני גר בפרברים עם
ha'iti gar ba'ir aval akhshav ani gar baparvarim im
I used to live in the city but now I I live in the suburbs with

המשפחה שלי.
hamishpakha sheli
the family my

(341) I usually wake up before my husband.

אני בדרך כלל מתעוררת לפני בעלי.
ani bederekh klal mitoreret lifnei ba'ali
I usually I wake up before my husband

(342) I visited England for the first time five years ago.

ביקרתי באנגליה בפעם הראשונה לפני חמש שנים.
bikarti be'angliya bapa'am harishona lifnei khamesh shanim
I visited / in England / in the time / the first / ago / five / years

(343) I want to take advantage of the nice weather and go for a long walk.

אני רוצה לנצל את מזג האוויר הנעים ולצאת
ani rotsa lenatsel et mezeg ha'avir hana'im velatset
I / I want / to take advantage of / D.O. / the weather / the nice / and to go out

להליכה ארוכה.
lehalikha aruka
for walk / long

(344) I want to be alone.

אני רוצה להיות לבד.
ani rotsa lihiyot levad
I / I want / to be / alone

(345) I want to clean the apartment thoroughly before our visitor arrives.

אני רוצה לנקות את הדירה ביסודיות לפני שהאורחת
ani rotsa lenakot et hadira bisodiyut lifnei sheha'orakhat
I / I want / to clean / D.O. / the apartment / thoroughly / before / that the visitor

שלנו מגיעה.
shelanu magi'a
our / she arrives

(346) I want to exchange this shirt for a smaller size. This one is too big.

אני רוצה להחליף את החולצה הזאת למידה קטנה יותר.
ani rotsa lehakhlif et hakhultsa hazot lemida ktana yoter
I / I want / to exchange / D.O. / the shirt / the this / for size / small / more

זאת גדולה מידי.
zot gdola midai
this / big / too

(347) I want to go on an inexpensive vacation. What do you advise?

אני רוצה לצאת לחופשה לא יקרה. מה אתה מייעץ?
ani rotsa latset lekhufsha lo yekara. ma ata meya'ets
I / I want / to go out / to vacation / not / expensive / what / you / you advise

(348) I was at the store the other day and ran into an old friend.

הייתי בחנות איזה יום ונתקלתי בחבר ותיק.
ha'iti bakhanut eize yom venitkalti bekhaver vatik
I was / at the store / the other day / and I bumped into / (at) friend / old

(349) I was in a car accident, but it wasn't my fault.

הייתי בתאונת דרכים, אבל זאת לא היתה אשמתי.
ha'iti bite'unat drakhim, aval zot lo haita ashmati
I was / in car accident / but / this / no / it was / my fault

(350) I was just about to call you.

בדיוק באתי להתקשר אליך.
bediyuk bati lehitkasher eleikha
I was just about to / to call / to you

(351) I was not happy with my job and quit.

לא הייתי מרוצה בעבודה והתפטרתי.
lo ha'iti merutse ba'avoda vehitpatarti
no / I was / satisfied / with the job / and I quit

I was sick yesterday, which is why I wasn't in the office. **(352)**

הייתי חולה אתמול, וזאת הסיבה שלא הייתי במשרד.

bamisrad	shelo ha'iti	hasiba	vezot	etmol	khole	ha'iti
in the office	that I was not	the reason	and this	yesterday	sick	I was

I was very happy to see you. Please visit again soon. **(353)**

שמחתי מאוד לראות אותך. בבקשה תבקרי שוב

shuv	tevakri	bevakasha	otakh	lirot	me'od	samakhti
again	you will visit	please	you	to see	very	I was happy

בקרוב.

bekarov
soon

I weigh too much. I should lose weight. **(354)**

אני שוקל יותר מידי. אני צריך להוריד במשקל.

lehorid bamishkal	tsarikh	ani	yoter midai	shokel	ani
to lose weight	I need	I	too much	I weigh	I

I will be there in five minutes. **(355)**

אני אהיה שם עוד חמש דקות.

dakot	khamesh	od	sham	eheye	ani
minutes	five	another	there	I will be	I

I will copy the files to the flash drive for you. **(356)**

אני אעתיק את הקבצים להחסן הנייד בשבילך.

bishvilkha	lahekhsen hanayad	hakvatsim	et	a'atik	ani
for you	to the flash drive	the files	D.O.	I will copy	I

I will definitely help you. You can count on me. **(357)**

בוודאי שאעזור לך. אתה יכול לסמוך עלי.

alai	lismokh	yakhol	ata	lekha	she'ezor	bevadai
on me	to rely	you can	you	to you	that I will help	definitely

I will give you another chance. **(358)**

אני אתן לך הזדמנות נוספת.

nosefet	hizdamnut	lakh	eten	ani
another	chance	to you	I will give	I

I will never be able to forgive him for what he did. **(359)**

אני לעולם לא אוכל לסלוח לו על מה שהוא עשה.

asa	shehu	ma	al	lo	lislo'akh	ukhal	le'olam lo	ani
he did	that he	what	for	to him	to forgive	I will be able	never	I

I will never come back to this restaurant. **(360)**

אני לעולם לא אחזור למסעדה הזאת.

hazot	lamisada	ekhzor	le'olam lo	ani
the this	to the restaurant	I will return	never	I

I won't let you treat me like this anymore. **(361)**

אני לא אתן לך להתייחס אלי ככה יותר.

yoter	kakha	elai	lehityakhes	lekha	eten	lo	ani
anymore	this way	(to) me	to treat	to you	I will let	no	I

I work part-time while also going to university. **(362)**

אני עובד במשרה חלקית, ובמקביל לומד

lomed	uvemakbil	khelkit	bemisra	oved	ani
I study	and at the same time	part-time	at job	I work	I

באוניברסיטה.

ba'universita
at the university

(363) I would like more information before I decide.

הייתי רוצה עוד מידע לפני שאני מחליט.
makhlit she'ani lifnei meida od ha'iti rotse
I decide that I before information more I would like

(364) I would like to come, but unfortunately I can't.

הייתי רוצה לבוא, אבל לצערי אני לא יכול.
yakhol lo ani letsa'ari aval lavo ha'iti rotse
I can no I unfortunately but to come I would like

(365) I want to eat something before we go.

אני רוצה לאכול משהו לפני שאנחנו יוצאים.
yotsim she'anakhnu lifnei mashehu le'ekhol rotse ani
we leave that we before something to eat I want I

(366) I would like to lose weight. Therefore I'm going on a diet.

הייתי רוצה להוריד במשקל. לכן אני מתחיל דיאטה.
di'eta matkhil ani lakhen lehorid bamishkal ha'iti rotse
diet I start I therefore to lose weight I would like

(367) I would like to work in an office instead of outside under the hot sun.

אני רוצה לעבוד בתוך משרד במקום בחוץ תחת השמש
hashemesh takhat bakhuts bimkom misrad betokh la'avod rotse ani
the sun under outside instead of office in to work I want I

הקופחת.
hakofakhat
the beating down

(368) If I were rich, I would go on a round-the-world trip.

אם הייתי עשיר, הייתי יוצא לטיול מסביב לעולם.
misaviv la'olam letiyul ha'iti yotse ashir ha'iti im
around the world on trip I would go rich I was if

(369) If it rains, we'll just have the party at our house instead of at the park.

אם ירד גשם, פשוט נקיים את המסיבה בבית
baba'it hamesiba et nekayem pashut geshem yered im
at the house the party D.O. we will perform just rain it will fall if

שלנו במקום בפארק.
bapark bimkom shelanu
at the park instead of our

(370) If it's supposed to rain, then you should bring an umbrella.

אם אמור לרדת גשם, אז כדאי שתביא
shetavi kedai az geshem laredet amur im
that you will bring worthwhile then rain to fall it is supposed to if

מטרייה.
mitriya
umbrella

(371) If the strawberries have gone bad, then you should throw them away.

אם התותים התקלקלו, אז כדאי שתזרוק
shetizrok kedai az hitkalkelu hatutim im
that you will throw away worthwhile then they spoiled the strawberries if

אותם.
otam
them

If the weather's nice, we could have a picnic.

(372) אם מזג האוויר נעים, אנחנו יכולים לעשות פיקניק.

im *mezeg ha'avir* *na'im* *anakhnu* *yekholim* *la'asot* *piknik*
if — the weather — nice — we — we could — to do — picnic

If we hurry, we can still watch the end of the game.

(373) אם נמהר, עדיין נוכל לצפות בסוף המשחק.

im *nemaher* *ada'in* *nukhal* *litspot* *besof* *hamiskhak*
if — we will hurry — still — we will be able — to watch — at end of — the game

---

If you do not pay the bill on time, you will receive an overdue notice.

(374) אם לא תשלם את החשבון בזמן, תקבל התראה

im *lo* *teshalem* *et* *hakheshbon* *bazman* *tekabel* *hatra'a*
if — no — you will pay — D.O. — the bill — on time — you will receive — warning

על אי תשלום.

al *i* *tashlum*
about — non — payment

If you drive drunk, you will go to jail.

(375) אם תנהגי שיכורה, את תלכי לכלא.

im *tinhagi* *shikora* *at* *telkhi* *lakele*
if — you will drive — drunk — you — you will go — to the jail

---

If you have any questions, go to the information desk.

(376) אם יש לך שאלות כלשהן, לך לדלפק המודיעין.

im *yesh lekha* *she'elot* *kolshehen* *lekh* *ledelpak* *hamodi'in*
if — you have — questions — any — go — to desk of — the information

---

If you have low income, you only pay a little tax.

(377) אם יש לך הכנסה נמוכה, אתה משלם רק מעט מס.

im *yesh lekha* *hakhnasa* *nemukha* *ata* *meshalem* *rak* *me'at* *mas*
if — you have — income — low — you — you pay — only — a little — tax

---

If you press here, the door opens.

(378) אם תלחץ פה, הדלת תיפתח.

im *tilkhats* *po* *hadelet* *tipatakh*
if — you will press — here — the door — it will be opened

If you spend more than you earn, then you won't save any money.

(379) אם אתה מוציא יותר ממה שאתה מכניס, אתה לא

im *ata* *motsi* *yoter* *mima* *she'ata* *makhnis* *ata* *lo*
if — you — you spend — more — than what — that you — you earn — you — no

תחסוך שום כסף.

takhsokh *shum* *kesef*
you will save — not any — money

If you want to open the file you have to click twice with the mouse.

(380) אם אתה רוצה לפתוח את הקובץ, אתה צריך להקיש

im *ata* *rotse* *lifto'akh* *et* *hakovets* *ata* *tsarikh* *lehakish*
if — you — you want — to open — D.O. — the file — you — you need — to click

פעמיים עם העכבר.

pa'ama'im *im* *ha'akhbar*
twice — with — the mouse

I'll be right back. This should take only a few minutes.

(381) מיד אשוב. זה צריך לקחת רק כמה דקות.

miyad *ashuv* *ze* *tsarikh* *lakakhat* *rak* *kama* *dakot*
promptly — I will return — this — it should — to take — only — a few — minutes

(382) I'll call you tonight.

אני אתקשר אליך הערב.

ha'erev eleikha etkasher ani
tonight to you I will call I

(383) I'll email you when I get there as soon as I have internet access.

אני אשלח לך מייל כשאני אגיע לשם, ברגע

barega lesham agi'a kshe'ani meil lekha eshlakh ani
as soon as to there I will arrive when I email to you I will send I

שתהיה לי גישה לרשת.

lareshet gisha shetihiye li
to the internet access that I will have

(384) I'll get you something to drink. You must be thirsty.

אני אביא לך משהו לשתות. אתה בטח צמא.

tsame betakh ata lishtot mashehu lekha avi ani
thirsty surely you to drink something to you I will bring I

(385) I'll give this to you for free. - Why? What's the catch?

אני אתן לך את זה בחינם. - למה? מה הקאץ'?

hakech ma lama bekhinam ze et lekha eten ani
the catch what why for free this D.O. to you I will give I

(386) I'll meet you at the café across from the school.

אני אפגוש אותך בבית הקפה שמול בית הספר.

beit hasefer shemul beveit hakafe otkha efgosh ani
the school that across from at the cafe you I will meet I

(387) I'll sell you the tomatoes for half price.

אני אמכור לך את העגבניות בחצי מחיר.

mekhir bekhatsi ha'agvaniyot et lekha emkor ani
price for half the tomatoes D.O. to you I will sell I

(388) I'll shovel the snow out of the driveway if you shovel the sidewalk.

אני אגרוף את השלג מכביש הגישה אם אתה

ata im mikvish hagisha hasheleg et egrof ani
you if from driveway the snow D.O. I will shovel I

תגרוף את המדרכה.

hamidrakha et tigrof
the sidewalk D.O. you will shovel

(389) I'll take you home.

אני אקח אותך הביתה.

habaita otkha ekakh ani
home you I will take I

(390) I'll transfer the money to you electronically.

אני אעביר לך את הכסף באופן אלקטרוני.

elektroni be'ofen hakesef et lekha a'avir ani
electronic in manner the money D.O. to you I will transfer I

(391) I'll wait for you in the car.

אני אחכה לך באוטו.

ba'oto lekha akhake ani
in the car for you I will wait I

(392) I'm already looking forward to my next vacation.

אני כבר מחכה לחופשה הבאה שלי.

sheli haba'a lakhufsha mekhaka kvar ani
my next to the vacation I look forward already I

I'm doing an internship at a company for three months this summer.

אני עושה התמחות בחברה למשך שלושה חודשים
ani	osa	hitmakhut	bekhevra	lemeshekh	shlosha	khodashim
I	I do	internship	at company	for	three	months

הקיץ.
haka'its
this summer

(393)

I feel better today, but yesterday I was in a really bad mood.

אני מרגיש יותר טוב היום, אבל אתמול הייתי ממש
ani	margish	yoter	tov	hayom	aval	etmol	ha'iti	mamash
I	I feel	more	good	today	but	yesterday	I was	really

מצוברח.
metsuvrakh
in a bad mood

(394)

I'm going out with my sisters tonight.

אני יוצא עם האחיות שלי הערב.
ani	yotse	im	ha'akhayot	sheli	ha'erev
I	I go out	with	the sisters	my	tonight

(395)

I'm happy that everything went so well.

אני שמח שהכל הסתדר כל כך יפה.
ani	same'akh	shehakol	histader	kol kakh	yafe
I	happy	that everything	it worked out	so	well

(396)

I'm learning Portuguese because I want to travel to Brazil.

אני לומד פורטוגלית כי אני רוצה לטייל בברזיל.
ani	lomed	portugalit	ki	ani	rotse	letayel	bebrazil
I	I learn	Portuguese	because	I	I want	to travel	in Brazil

(397)

I'm learning to play guitar. I practice an hour per day.

אני לומד לנגן בגיטרה. אני מתרגל שעה ביום.
ani	lomed	lenagen	begitara	ani	metargel	sha'a	beyom
I	I learn	to play	(at) guitar	I	I practice	hour	per day

(398)

I'm looking for a car seat for my three year old son.

אני מחפש כיסא לרכב לבני בן השלוש.
ani	mekhapes	kise larekhev	livni	ben	hashalosh
I	I look for	for car seat	for my son	aged	the three

(399)

I'm looking for a low-priced vacation home.

אני מחפש בית חופשה במחיר נמוך.
ani	mekhapes	beit	khufsha	bimkhir	namukh
I	I look for	house of	vacation	for price	low

(400)

I'm looking for a used car that doesn't cost more than 3000 Euro.

אני מחפש מכונית משומשת שלא תעלה יותר
ani	mekhapes	mekhonit	meshumeshet	shelo	ta'ale	yoter
I	I look for	car	used	that no	it will cost	more

מ-3000 אירו.
mishloshet alafim *yuro*
than 3000 Euro

(401)

I'm looking for an apartment with three bedrooms.

אני מחפש דירה עם שלושה חדרי שינה.
ani	mekhapes	dira	im	shlosha	khadrei	sheina
I	I look for	apartment	with	three	rooms of	sleep

(402)

(403) I'm not interested in philosophy, but I'm interested in physics.

אני לא מתעניין בפילוסופיה, אבל אני מתעניין
ani lo mitanyen befilosofya, aval ani mitanyen
I no I am interested in philosophy but I I am interested

בפיזיקה.
befizika
in physics

(404) I'm on vacation until the end of August.

אני בחופשה עד סוף אוגוסט.
ani bekhufsha ad sof ogust
I on vacation until end of August

(405) I'm out of money. May I borrow some?

נגמר לי הכסף. אני יכול ללוות קצת?
nigmar li hakesef ani yakhol lilvot ktsat
I'm out of the money I I can to borrow a little

(406) I'm quite nervous. My heart is pounding.

אני די עצבני. הלב שלי דופק בחוזקה.
ani dei atsbani halev sheli dofek bekhozka
I quite nervous the heart my it beats strongly

(407) I'm seriously considering whether I should move to another city.

אני שוקל ברצינות אם כדאי לי לעבור לעיר אחרת.
ani shokel birtsinut im kedai li la'avor le'ir akheret
I I consider seriously if worthwhile to me to move to city another

(408) I'm starting to doubt my boss's leadership skills.

אני מתחיל להטיל ספק בכישורי ההנהגה של המנהל
ani matkhil lehatil safek bekishurei hahanhaga shel hamenahel
I I start to cast doubt at skills of leadership of the boss

שלי.
sheli
my

(409) I'm staying home until the package is delivered.

אני נשאר בבית עד שימסרו את החבילה.
ani nishar baba'it ad she'imseru et hakhavila
I I stay at home until that it will be delivered D.O. the package

(410) I'm used to waking up early because I have kids.

אני רגיל לקום מוקדם כי יש לי ילדים.
ani ragil lakum mukdam ki yesh li yeladim
I used to to wake up early because I have kids

(411) I'm working from home today.

אני עובד מהבית היום.
ani oved mehaba'it hayom
I I work from the house today

(412) In autumn we gather mushrooms in the forest.

בסתיו אנחנו מלקטים פטריות ביער.
bastav anakhnu melaktim pitriyot baya'ar
in the autumn we we gather mushrooms in the forest

(413) In chess, each player has sixteen pieces.

בשח-מט, לכל שחקן יש שישה עשר כלים.
beshakh-mat, lekhol sakhkan yesh shisha asar kelim
in chess to every player there is sixteen pieces

In general I am very satisfied with my job.

בכללי אני מאוד מרוצה מהעבודה שלי. (414)

baklali *ani* *me'od* *merutse* *meha'avoda* *sheli*
in general I very satisfied of the job my

In Iceland there are only three hot days per year.

באיסלנד יש רק שלושה ימים חמים בשנה. (415)

be'island *yesh* *rak* *shlosha* *yamim* *khamim* *beshana*
in Iceland there are only three days hot per year

In my free time I am learning to play the violin.

בזמני החופשי אני לומד לנגן בכינור. (416)

bizmani *hakhofshi* *ani* *lomed* *lenagen* *bekhinor*
in my time the free I I learn to play (at) violin

In my psychology class there are more women than men.

בשיעור הפסיכולוגיה שלי יש יותר נשים מגברים. (417)

beshi'ur *hapsikhologya* *sheli* *yesh* *yoter* *nashim* *migvarim*
in class of the psychology my there are more women than men

In order to vote, please go into this booth.

על מנת להצביע, אנא הכנסי לתא הזה. (418)

al menat *lehatsbi'a* *ana* *hikansi* *lata* *haze*
in order to to vote please enter to the booth the this

In soccer, there are eleven players on the field for each team.

בכדורגל, יש אחד עשר שחקנים במגרש לכל (419)

bekhaduregel *yesh* *akhad asar* *sakhkanim* *bamigrash* *lekhol*
in soccer there are eleven players on the field for each

קבוצה.

kvutsa
team

In Spain it is common to eat late at night.

בספרד נפוץ שאוכלים מאוחר בלילה. (420)

bisfarad *nafots* *she'okhlim* *me'ukhar* *balaila*
in Spain common that they eat late at night

In the summer you should not go out into the sun without wearing sunscreen.

בקיץ לא כדאי לצאת לשמש בלי למרוח (421)

baka'its *lo* *kedai* *latset* *lashemesh* *bli* *limro'akh*
in the summer not worthwhile to go out into the sun without to apply

קרם הגנה.

krem *hagana*
cream of defense

In this market you can negotiate and get things cheaper.

בשוק הזה אתה יכול להתמקח ולהשיג דברים (422)

bashuk *haze* *ata* *yakhol* *lehitmake'akh* *ulehasig* *dvarim*
in the market the this you you can to negotiate and to get things

בזול יותר.

bezol *yoter*
for cheap more

Is the ring made of gold? - Sort of, it's gold-plated.

הטבעת עשויה מזהב? - בערך, היא מצופה בזהב. (423)

hataba'at *asuya* *mizahav* *be'erekh* *hi* *metsupa* *bezahav*
the ring made of of gold sort of it plated in gold

41

(424) Is your cell phone broken? We'll send it back to the manufacturer and have it repaired.

בחזרה אותו נשלח שבור? שלך הנייד
bakhazara *oto* *nishlakh* *shavur* *shelkha* *hanayad*
back to · it · we will send · broken · your · the cell phone

ליצרן לתיקון.
letikun *layatsran*
for repair · to the manufacturer

(425) It is better to give than to receive.

טוב יותר לתת מאשר לקבל.
lekabel *me'asher* *latet* *yoter* *tov*
to receive · than · to give · more · good

(426) It is cold outside.

קר בחוץ.
bakhuts *kar*
outside · cold

(427) It is exactly eight o'clock.

השעה בדיוק שמונה.
shmone *bediyuk* *hasha'a*
eight · exactly · the hour

(428) It is so dark in this room. Where is the light switch?

כל כך חשוך בחדר הזה. איפה המפסק של האור?
ha'or *shel* *hamafsek* *eifo* *haze* *bakheder* *khashukh* *kol kakh*
the light · of · the switch · where · the this · in the room · dark · so

(429) It is very kind of you to pick me up.

יפה מצדך לאסוף אותי.
oti *le'esof* *mitsidkha* *yafe*
me · to pick up · of you · nice

(430) It just stopped raining, and now there is a rainbow.

בדיוק הפסיק לרדת גשם, ועכשיו יש קשת בענן.
keshet be'anan *yesh* *ve'akhshav* *geshem* *laredet* *hifsik* *bediyuk*
rainbow · there is · and now · rain · to fall · it stopped · just

(431) It rained, so I don't need to water my garden.

ירד גשם, אז אני לא צריך להשקות את הגינה שלי.
sheli *hagina* *et* *lehashkot* *tsarikh* *lo* *ani* *az* *geshem* *yarad*
my · the garden · D.O. · to water · I need · no · I · so · rain · it fell

(432) It takes a lot of courage to start a new life in a foreign country.

צריך המון אומץ להתחיל חיים חדשים במדינה זרה.
zara *bimdina* *khadashim* *khayim* *lehatkhil* *omets* *hamon* *tsarikh*
foreign · in country · new · life · to start · courage · a lot of · it requires

(433) It takes me about ten minutes to drive to work.

לוקח לי בערך עשר דקות לנהוג לעבודה.
la'avoda *linhog* *dakot* *eser* *be'erekh* *li* *loke'akh*
to the work · to drive · minutes · ten · about · for me · it takes

(434) It was a great concert. The audience was really enthusiastic.

זאת היתה הופעה נהדרת. הקהל היה ממש נלהב.
nilhav *mamash* *haya* *hakahal* *nehederet* *hofa'a* *haita* *zot*
enthusiastic · really · it was · the audience · great · concert · it was · it

It's strange that my brother isn't here yet. He is usually so punctual.

(435) מוזר שאחי עדיין לא פה. הוא בדרך כלל מדייק.
muzar she'akhi ada'in lo po hu bederekh klal medayek
strange that my brother still not here he usually punctual

It's stuffy in here. Please open the window.

(436) חנוק פה. בבקשה תפתח את החלון.
khanuk po bevakasha tiftakh et hakhalon
stuffy here please you will open D.O. the window

I've been awake for two hours already.

(437) אני ער כבר שעתיים.
ani er kvar sha'ata'im
I awake already two hours

I've had a sore throat since yesterday.

(438) הגרון כואב לי מאתמול.
hagaron ko'ev li me'etmol
the throat it hurts to me from yesterday

I've never heard that expression.

(439) מעולם לא שמעתי את הביטוי הזה.
me'olam lo shamati et habitui haze
never I heard D.O. the expression the that

Just ask my girlfriend. She always has good ideas.

(440) פשוט תשאל את חברה שלי. תמיד יש לה רעיונות טובים.
pashut tishal et khavera sheli tamid yesh la ra'ayonot tovim
just you will ask D.O. girlfriend my always she has ideas good

Karl is already over 60. But he is still very fit.

(441) קארל כבר מעל גיל 60. אבל הוא עדיין מאוד בכושר.
karl kvar me'al gil shishim aval hu ada'in me'od bekosher
Karl already over age sixty but he still very in shape

Let me know as soon as possible, please.

(442) תודיע לי בהקדם האפשרי, בבקשה.
todi'a li bahekdem ha'efshari bevakasha
you will inform to me as soon as possible please

Let's eat dinner on the balcony.

(443) בוא נאכל ארוחת ערב במרפסת.
bo nokhal arukhat erev bamirpeset
let's we will eat meal of evening on the balcony

Look at the camera and smile!

(444) תסתכל על המצלמה ותחייך!
tistakel al hamatslema vetekhayekh
you will look at the camera and you will smile

Look both ways before crossing the street.

(445) תסתכל לשני הכיוונים לפני שאתה חוצה את הרחוב.
tistakel lishnei hakivunim lifnei she'ata khotse et harekhov
you will look to both directions before that you you cross D.O. the street

Making mistakes is quite normal.

(446) זה די נורמאלי לעשות טעויות.
ze dei normali la'asot ta'uyot
it quite normal to make mistakes

(447) Many artists and musicians live in this neighborhood.

המון אומנים ומוזיקאים גרים בשכונה הזאת.
hamon omanim umuzika'im garim bashkhuna hazot
many artists and musicians they live in the neighborhood the this

(448) Many immigrants come from India.

המון מהגרים מגיעים מהודו.
hamon mehagrim magi'im mehodu
many immigrants they arrive from India

(449) Many words have several meanings.

להרבה מילים יש מספר משמעויות.
leharbe milim yesh mispar mashma'uyot
for many words there are several meanings

(450) Marco speaks four languages.

מרקו מדבר ארבע שפות.
marko medaber arba safot
Marco he speaks four languages

(451) Maria is very intelligent and is very good at mathematics.

מריה מאוד אינטליגנטית ומאוד טובה במתמטיקה.
mariya me'od inteligentit ume'od tova bematematika
Maria very intelligent and very good at mathematics

(452) May I borrow your phone charger? My battery died.

אני יכול לשאול את מטען הנייד שלך? הסוללה
ani yakhol lishol et maten hanayad shelkha hasolela
I I can to borrow D.O. charger of the cell phone your the battery

שלי נגמרה.
sheli nigmera
my it ran out

(453) Men and women have equal rights - at least they do in my country.

גברים ונשים הם בעלי אותן זכויות - לפחות כך
gvarim venashim hem ba'alei otan zkhuyot lefakhot kakh
men and women they having same rights at least like this

זה במדינה שלי.
ze bamedina sheli
this in the country my

(454) Messi is a famous soccer player.

מסי הוא שחקן כדורגל מפורסם.
mesi hu sakhkan kaduregel mefursam
Messi he player of soccer famous

(455) Michael has been absent from school for three days.

מייקל נעדר מבית הספר למשך שלושה ימים.
maikel ne'edar mibeit hasefer lemeshekh shlosha yamim
Michael he was absent from school for three days

(456) Mike has a beard now. He looks much older.

למייק יש זקן עכשיו. הוא נראה ממש מבוגר יותר.
lemaik yesh zakan akhshav hu nire mamash mevugar yoter
Mike has beard now he he looks much older more

(457) Mo drives his motorcycle to work every day.

מו רוכב על האופנוע שלו לעבודה כל יום.
mo rokhev al ha'ofno'a shelo la'avoda kol yom
Mo he drives on the motorcycle his to the work every day

Mom cut her finger while chopping garlic.

(458) אמא חתכה לעצמה את האצבע תוך שהיא קוצצת שום.

shum	kotsetset	shehi	tokh	ha'etsba	et	le'atsma	khatkha	ima
garlic	she chops	that she	while	the finger	D.O.	herself	she cut	mom

Monday is a national holiday.

(459) ביום שני חל יום חג לאומי.

le'umi	yom khag	khal	beyom sheni
national	holiday	it occurs	on Monday

More than two hundred guests are coming to the wedding.

(460) יותר ממאתיים אורחים באים לחתונה.

lakhatuna	ba'im	orkhim	mimata'im	yoter
to the wedding	they come	guests	than two hundred	more

Most people don't realize that doctors usually aren't experts in nutrition.

(461) רוב האנשים אינם מבינים שרופאים בדרך כלל

bederekh klal	sherofim	mevinim	einam	ha'anashim	rov
usually	that doctors	they are aware	they are not	the people	most

אינם מומחים בתזונה.

bitzuna	mumkhim	einam
in nutrition	experts	they are not

Most scientists say climate change is the fault of humans.

(462) רוב המדענים אומרים ששינוי האקלים הוא באשמת

be'ashmat	hu	ha'aklim	sheshinui	omrim	hamadanim	rov
(by) fault of	it	the climate	that change of	they say	the scientists	most

בני האדם.

bnei ha'adam
the humans

My baby knows how to use a spoon.

(463) התינוק שלי יודע איך להשתמש בכפית.

bekhapit	lehishtamesh	eikh	yode'a	sheli	hatinok
(with) small spoon	to use	how	he knows	my	the baby

My boy used to love those toys, but he doesn't care about them anymore.

(464) הבן שלי אהב את הצעצועים האלה, אבל לא אכפת לו

ikhpat lo	lo	aval	ha'ele	hatsa'atsu'im	et	ahav	sheli	haben
he cares	no	but	the those	the toys	D.O.	he loved	my	the son

מהם יותר.

yoter	mehem
anymore	about them

My brother is a very tidy person, while my sister is a slob.

(465) אחי הוא איש מאוד מסודר, בעוד שאחותי

she'akhoti	be'od	mesudar	me'od	ish	hu	akhi
that my sister	while	tidy	very	person	he	my brother

מרושלת.

merushelet
sloppy

My brother is three years younger than me.

(466) אחי צעיר ממני בשלוש שנים.

shanim	beshalosh	mimeni	tsa'ir	akhi
years	by three	then me	younger	my brother

(467) My brother never answers his phone when I call.

אחי אף פעם לא עונה לטלפון כשאני מתקשר.
akhi af pa'am lo one latelefon kshe'ani mitkasher
my brother never no he answers to the telephone when I I call

(468) My car is brand new. I just bought it yesterday.

המכונית שלי חדשה דנדשה. רק אתמול קניתי אותה.
hamekhonit sheli khadasha dandasha rak etmol kaniti ota
the car my new brand just yesterday I bought it

(469) My children are very diligent. They always do their homework right when they get home.

הילדים שלי מאוד שקדנים. הם תמיד מכינים את
hayeladim sheli me'od shakdanim hem tamid mekhinim et
the children my very diligent they always they do D.O.

שיעורי הבית שלהם ברגע שהם מגיעים הביתה.
shi'urei haba'it shelahem barega shehem magi'im habaita
the homework their at the moment that they they arrive home

(470) My colleague strongly believes that he deserves a promotion.

עמית שלי לעבודה מאמין בתוקף שמגיע לו קידום.
amit sheli la'avoda ma'amin betokef shemagi'a lo kidum
colleague my at the work he believes firmly that he deserves promotion

(471) My daughter never wants my advice.

הבת שלי אף פעם לא מעוניינת בעצה ממני.
habat sheli af pa'am lo me'unyenet be'etsa mimeni
the daughter my never no she is interested in advice from me

(472) My daughter starts high school next year.

הבת שלי מתחילה תיכון בשנה הבאה.
habat sheli matkhila tikhon bashana haba'a
the daughter my she starts high school in the year next

(473) My favorite drink is fresh-squeezed orange juice.

המשקה האהוב עלי הוא מיץ תפוזים סחוט טרי.
hamashke ha'ahuv alai hu mits tapuzim sakhut tari
the drink the favorite for me it juice of oranges squeezed fresh

(474) My flight was canceled because of bad weather.

הטיסה שלי בוטלה עקב תנאי מזג אויר קשים.
hatisa sheli butla ekev tna'ei mezeg avir kashim
the flight my it was canceled due to conditions of weather severe

(475) My girlfriend is a caregiver in a retirement home.

החברה שלי מטפלת בבית אבות.
hakhavera sheli metapelet beveit avot
the girlfriend my caregiver at retirement home

(476) My grandfather is not working anymore. He is retired.

סבא שלי לא עובד יותר. הוא פרש.
saba sheli lo oved yoter hu parash
grandfather my no he works anymore he he is retired

(477) My grandma can't climb stairs anymore.

סבתא שלי לא יכולה לטפס במדרגות יותר.
savta sheli lo yekhola letapes bamadregot yoter
grandmother my no she can to climb by stairs anymore

My grandma just turned 85.

(478)	סבתא	שלי	בדיוק	חגגה	85.
	savta	*sheli*	*bediyuk*	*khagega*	*shmonim vekhamesh*
	grandmother	my	just	she celebrated	eighty-five

My grandmother told us interesting stories of her youth.

(479)	סבתא	שלי	סיפרה	לנו	סיפורים	מעניינים	מימי
	savta	*sheli*	*sipra*	*lanu*	*sipurim*	*me'anyenim*	*miymei*
	grandmother	my	she told	to us	stories	interesting	from days of

צעירותה.
tse'iruta
her youth

My grandparents died many years ago, but I can still remember them well.

(480)	הסבא	והסבתא	שלי	מתו	לפני	שנים	רבות,
	hasaba	*vehasavta*	*sheli*	*metu*	*lifnei*	*shanim*	*rabot*
	the grandfather	and the grandmother	my	they died	ago	years	many

אבל אני עדיין זוכר אותם היטב.
aval ani ada'in zokher otam heitev
but I still I remember them well

My mother got flowers and chocolate for her birthday.

(481)	אמא	שלי	קיבלה	פרחים	ושוקולד	ליום ההולדת	שלה.
	ima	*sheli*	*kibla*	*prakhim*	*veshokolad*	*leyom hahuledet*	*shela*
	mother	my	she received	flowers	and chocolate	for the birthday	her

My mother has been running her own business for twenty years.

(482)	אמא	שלי	מנהלת	עסק	משלה	זה	עשרים	שנה.
	ima	*sheli*	*menahelet*	*esek*	*mishela*	*ze*	*esrim*	*shana*
	mother	my	she manages	business	of her own	since	twenty	years

My mother's family is very big, so I have many aunts and uncles.

(483)	המשפחה	של	אמא	שלי	מאוד	גדולה,	לכן	יש לי	המון
	hamishpakha	*shel*	*ima*	*sheli*	*me'od*	*gdola*	*lakhen*	*yesh li*	*hamon*
	the family	of	mother	my	very	big	so	I have	many

דודות ודודים.
dodot vedodim
aunts and uncles

My neighbor is moving out next month. Are you still interested in the apartment?

(484)	השכן	שלי	עוזב	בחודש	הבא.	אתה	עדיין
	hashakhen	*sheli*	*ozev*	*bakhodesh*	*haba*	*ata*	*ada'in*
	the neighbor	my	he moves	in the month	next	you	still

מעוניין בדירה?
me'unyan badira
you are interested in the apartment

My other daughter is an engineer.

(485)	הבת	האחרת	שלי	מהנדסת.
	habat	*ha'akheret*	*sheli*	*mehandeset*
	the daughter	the other	my	engineer

My parents died many years ago.

(486)	הוריי	מתו	לפני	הרבה	שנים.
	horai	*metu*	*lifnei*	*harbe*	*shanim*
	my parents	they died	ago	many	years

My passport is valid for only two more months, so I should renew it immediately. (487)

הדרכון שלי בתוקף רק לעוד חודשיים, לכן כדאי
kedai lakhen khodsha'im le'od rak betokef sheli hadarkon
worthwhile so two months for another only valid my the passport

שאני אחדש אותו מידית.
miyadit oto akhadesh she'ani
immediately it I will renew that I

My siblings have nine children in total. (488)

לאחיי ולאחיותיי יש סך הכל תשעה ילדים.
yeladim tisha sakh hakol yesh ule'akhyotai le'akhai
children nine in total there are and to my sisters to my brothers

My sister has dark hair, whereas I have blond hair. (489)

לאחותי יש שיער כהה, בעוד שלי יש שיער בלונדיני.
blondini sei'ar sheli yesh be'od kehe sei'ar le'akhoti yesh
blond hair that I have whereas dark hair my sister has

My sister is interested in politics, but I am not interested in it. (490)

אחותי מתעניינת בפוליטיקה, אבל אני לא מתעניין
mitanyen lo ani aval bepolitika mitanyenet akhoti
I am interested no I but in politics she is interested my sister

בזה.
beze
in it

My son has grown a lot. He is already taller than me. (491)

הבן שלי גדל המון. הוא כבר גבוה ממני.
mimeni gavoha kvar hu hamon gadal sheli haben
than me tall already he a lot he grew my the son

My son is very thin. He eats too little. (492)

הבן שלי מאוד רזה. הוא אוכל מעט מידי.
midai me'at okhel hu raze me'od sheli haben
too little he eats he thin very my the son

My son paints very well. He has a lot of imagination. (493)

הבן שלי מצייר מאוד טוב. יש לו המון דמיון.
dimyon hamon yesh lo tov me'od metsayer sheli haben
imagination lots of he has well very he paints my the son

My son simply drove away with the car without asking my permission. (494)

הבן שלי פשוט נסע עם המכונית בלי לבקש ממני
mimeni levakesh bli hamekhonit im nasa pashut sheli haben
from me to ask without the car with he drove simply my the son

רשות.
reshut
permission

My son wants to study medicine and become a doctor like his mother. (495)

הבן שלי רוצה ללמוד רפואה ולהיות רופא כמו אמא
ima kmo rofe ulihiyot refu'a lilmod rotse sheli haben
mother like doctor and to be medicine to study he wants my the son

שלו.
shelo
his

My wife is three months pregnant.

(496) אשתי בהריון בחודש השלישי.
hashlishi *bakhodesh* *beherayon* *ishti*
the third in the month pregnant my wife

My youngest girl is four years old.

(497) בתי הצעירה בת ארבע.
arba *bat* *hatse'ira* *biti*
four age the young my girl

Normally I have to work on Monday, but today is an exception.

(498) בדרך כלל אני צריך לעבוד ביום שני, אבל היום זה
ze *hayom* *aval* *beyom sheni* *la'avod* *tsarikh* *ani* *bederekh klal*
this today but on Monday to work I need I normally

יוצא דופן.
yotse dofen
out of the ordinary

Of course I will help you. You are my friend after all.

(499) בוודאי שאעזור לך. אחרי הכל אתה חבר שלי.
sheli *khaver* *ata* *akharei hakol* *lekha* *she'e'ezor* *bevadai*
my friend you after all to you that I will help of course

On Sunday we're having a party. I still have to prepare a lot for it.

(500) אנחנו עושים מסיבה ביום ראשון. אני עדיין צריך לעשות
la'asot *tsarikh* *ada'in* *ani* *beyom rishon* *mesiba* *osim* *anakhnu*
to do I need still I on Sunday party we make we

המון הכנות.
hakhanot *hamon*
preparations a lot of

On the one hand I would like to take the trip, on the other hand it is too expensive for me.

(501) מצד אחד אני רוצה לצאת לטיול, מצד שני הטיול
hatiyul *mitsad sheni* *letiyul* *latset* *rotse* *ani* *mitsad ekhad*
the trip on the other hand on trip to go I want I on one hand

יקר לי מידי.
midai *li* *yakar*
too for me expensive

On the second day we took a tour through the harbor.

(502) ביום השני עשינו סיור דרך הנמל.
hanamal *derekh* *siyur* *asinu* *hasheni* *bayom*
the harbor through tour we did the second on the day

One can no longer imagine a world without internet.

(503) אי אפשר עוד לדמיין עולם בלי אינטרנט.
internet *bli* *olam* *ledamyen* *od* *efshar* *i*
internet without world to imagine anymore possible not

One has an amazing view of the city from this tower.

(504) יש נוף מדהים של העיר מהמגדל הזה.
haze *mehamigdal* *ha'ir* *shel* *madhim* *nof* *yesh*
the this from the tower the city of amazing view there is

Originally I wanted to be a doctor, but instead I became a dentist.

במקור רציתי להיות רופא, אבל נהייתי רופא שיניים
bamakor ratsiti lihiyot rofe aval nihiyeti rofe shina'im
originally I wanted to be doctor but I became doctor of teeth

במקום.
bimkom
instead

(505)

Our business is going well. Our revenues were higher this month than last.

העסק שלנו הולך טוב. ההכנסות שלנו החודש
ha'esek shelanu holekh tov hahakhnasot shelanu hakhodesh
the business our it goes well the revenues our this month

גבוהות מבחודש שעבר.
gvohot mibekhodesh she'avar
high from in month past

(506)

Our company has only seven employees.

יש בחברה שלנו שבעה עובדים בלבד.
yesh bakhevra shelanu shiva ovdim bilvad
there are in the company our seven employees only

(507)

Our dog's hair is all over the house.

השערות של הכלב שלנו מפוזרות בכל הבית.
hase'arot shel hakelev shelanu mefuzarot bekhol haba'it
the hairs of the dogs our they are scattered in all the house

(508)

Our friend's child has been disabled since the accident.

הילדה של ידיד שלנו נכה מאז התאונה.
hayalda shel yadid shelanu nekha me'az hate'una
the child of friend our disabled since the accident

(509)

Our neighbor is very polite. He always says good morning.

השכן שלנו מאוד מנומס. הוא תמיד אומר בוקר
hashakhen shelanu me'od menumas hu tamid omer boker
the neighbor our very polite he always he says morning

טוב.
tov
good

(510)

Our rent is very high, but the location is good.

השכירות שלנו מאוד גבוהה, אבל המיקום טוב.
haskhirut shelanu me'od gvoha aval hamikum tov
the rent our very high but the location good

(511)

Our two children are very different from each other.

שני ילדינו מאוד שונים זה מזה.
shnei yeladeinu me'od shonim ze mize
two of our children very different from each other

(512)

Our windows are not airtight. There is always a draft.

החלונות שלנו לא אטומים. תמיד יש רוח פרצים.
hakhalonot shelanu lo atumim tamid yesh ru'akh pratsim
the windows our not sealed always there is draft

(513)

Pardon me? What did you say?

סליחה? מה אמרת?
slikha ma amart
pardon me what you said

(514)

Paris is the capital of France.

פריז היא בירת צרפת. (515)
tsarfat birat hi pariz
France capital of it Paris

Parliament has enacted a new law.

בית המחוקקים חוקק חוק חדש. (516)
khadash khok khokek beit hamekhokekim
new law it legislated parliament

People in every country grumble about the weather.

בכל מדינה אנשים מקטרים על מזג האוויר. (517)
mezeg ha'avir al mekatrim anashim medina bekhol
the weather about they grumble people country in every

Picasso is perhaps the most famous painter in the world.

פיקסו הוא אולי הצייר המפורסם בעולם. (518)
ba'olam hamefursam hatsayar ulai hu pikaso
in the world the famous the painter perhaps he Picasso

Pick up your clothes off the floor.

תרים את הבגדים שלך מהרצפה. (519)
meharitspa shelkha habgadim et tarim
from the floor your the clothes D.O. you will pick up

Please bring me a cup of hot chocolate.

בבקשה תביא לי כוס שוקו חם. (520)
shoko kham kos li tavi bevakasha
hot chocolate cup of to me you will bring please

Please do not throw recycling in the normal garbage.

לפח למחזור אשפה תזרוק אל בבקשה (521)
lapakh lemikhzur ashpa tizrok al bevakasha
into the garbage can for recycling garbage you will throw don't please

הרגיל.
haragil
the regular

Please don't disturb me now. I have to concentrate on my work.

להתרכז אני צריך עכשיו. לי תפריע אל בבקשה (522)
lehitrakez tsarikh ani akhshav li tafri'a al bevakasha
to concentrate I need I now to me you will disturb don't please

בעבודה.
ba'avoda
on the work

Please get to the airport at least one hour before takeoff.

לפני שעה לפחות לנמל התעופה תגיע בבקשה (523)
lifnei sha'a lefakhot linmal hate'ufa tagi'a bevakasha
before hour at least to the airport you will arrive please

ההמראה.
hahamra'a
the takeoff

Please justify your opinion.

אנא תן צידוק לדעתך. (524)
leda'atkha tsiduk ten ana
for your opinion justification give please

51

Please knock on the door before entering.

אנא דפוק בדלת לפני שאתה נכנס. (525)
nikhnas she'ata lifnei badelet dfok ana
you enter that you before on the door knock please

Please read this information carefully.

בבקשה קרא מידע זה בתשומת לב. (526)
bitsumat lev ze meida kra bevakasha
with attention this information read please

Please remain seated during takeoff.

אנא הישארו ישובים בזמן ההמראה. (527)
hahamra'a bizman yeshuvim hisha'aru ana
the takeoff during seated remain please

Please remember to turn off the heating before you go to sleep.

בבקשה תזכרו לכבות את החימום לפני שאתם (528)
she'atem lifnei hakhimum et lekhabot tizkeru bevakasha
that you before the heating D.O. to turn off you will remember please

הולכים לישון.
lishon holkhim
to sleep you go

Please set your phone to vibrate or silent.

אנא שימו את הנייד במצב רטט או שקט. (529)
shaket o retet bematsav hanayad et simu ana
silent or vibrating at status of the cell phone D.O. put please

Please wash your hands before holding the baby.

בבקשה שטוף את הידיים לפני שתחזיק את (530)
et shetakhzik lifnei hayada'im et shtof bevakasha
D.O. that you will hold before the hands D.O. wash please

התינוקת.
hatinoket
the baby

Potatoes can be cooked many different ways.

אפשר לבשל תפוחי אדמה בדרכים רבות. (531)
rabot bidrakhim tapukhei adama levashel efshar
many in ways potatoes to cook possible

Put the milk in the fridge. Don't leave it on the counter.

שים את החלב במקרר. אל תשאיר אותו על (532)
al oto tashir al bamekarer hakhalav et sim
on it you will leave don't in the refrigerator the milk D.O. put

השיש.
hasha'ish
the counter

Read the contract before signing.

קרא את החוזה לפני שתחתום. (533)
shetakhtom lifnei hakhoze et kra
that you will sign before the contract D.O. read

Read the instructions before assembling the table.

קרא את ההוראות לפני שתרכיב את השולחן. (534)
hashulkhan et shetarkiv lifnei hahora'ot et kra
the table D.O. that you will assemble before the instructions D.O. read

Recently the economy has picked up again.	לאחרונה *la'akharona* recently	המצב *hamatsav* the situation	הכלכלי *hakalkali* the economic	חזר *khazar* it returned	להשתפר. *lehishtaper* to improve	(535)

Religion is very important to some people.	הדת *hadat* the religion	מאוד *me'od* very	חשובה *khashuva* important	לחלק *lekhelek* to some	מהאנשים. *meha'anashim* of the people	(536)

Rents are very high in this area.	השכירות *haskhirut* the rents	מאוד *me'od* very	גבוהה *gvoha* high	באזור *ba'ezor* in the area	הזה. *haze* the this	(537)

Round-trip? - No, just one-way please.

הלוך ושוב? - לא, רק כיוון אחד בבקשה. (538)
halokh vashov round-trip, *lo* no, *rak* just, *kivun* direction, *ekhad* one, *bevakasha* please

Sara filled her bucket with sand using a plastic shovel.

שרה מילאה את הדלי שלה בחול באמצעות את (539)
sara Sara, *mila* she filled, *et* D.O., *hadli* the bucket, *shela* her, *bekhol* with sand, *be'emtsa'ut* using, *et* shovel

מפלסטיק.
miplastik of plastic

Sara indeed wants to study, but on the other hand, she wants to earn money right away.

אכן שרה רוצה ללמוד, אבל מצד שני, היא רוצה (540)
akhen indeed, *sara* Sara, *rotsa* she wants, *lilmod* to study, *aval* but, *mitsad sheni* on the other hand, *hi* she, *rotsa* she wants

להרוויח כסף מיד.
leharvi'akh to earn, *kesef* money, *miyad* immediately

Scientists are trying to find a cure for cancer.

מדענים מנסים למצוא תרופה לסרטן. (541)
madanim scientists, *menasim* they try, *limtso* to find, *trufa* cure, *lesartan* for cancer

Shall we go grocery shopping and cook together afterwards? - Yes, that sounds good.

רוצה שנלך לקניות ושנבשל יחד (542)
rotsa you want, *shenelekh* that we will go, *likniyot* to shopping, *veshenevashel* and that we will cook, *yakhad* together

אחר כך? - כן, נשמע טוב.
akhar kakh afterwards, *ken* yes, *nishma* it sounds, *tov* good

Shall we go to the zoo with the kids on Saturday?

שנלך לגן החיות עם הילדים ביום שבת? (543)
shenelekh should we go, *legan hakhayot* to the zoo, *im* with, *hayeladim* the kids, *beyom shabat* on Saturday

She goes for a swim almost every day in the indoor swimming pool.

היא שוחה כמעט כל יום בבריכה המקורה. (544)
hi she, *sokha* she swims, *kimat* almost, *kol* every, *yom* day, *babreikha* in the swimming pool, *hamekura* the roofed

53

She has been my customer for a long time. I gave her a special price.

(545) היא לקוחה שלי זה זמן רב. נתתי לה מחיר מיוחד.

meyukhad mekhir la natati rav zman ze sheli lakokha hi
special price to her I gave much time since my customer she

She has two children from her first marriage.

(546) יש לה שני ילדים מהנישואין הראשונים.

harishonim mehanisu'in yeladim shnei yesh la
the first from the marriage children two of she has

She heard a strange noise in the attic.

(547) היא שמעה רעש מוזר בעליית הגג.

be'aliyat hagag muzar ra'ash shama hi
in the attic strange noise she heard she

She looked out the window of the train as it passed through the countryside.

(548) היא התבוננה מחלון הרכבת בעוד זו חולפת

kholefet zo be'od harakevet mekhalon hitbonena hi
it passed through it while the train from window of she looked out she

באזור הכפרי.

hakafri ba'ezor
the rural in the area of

She talked a lot, but her husband didn't say a word all evening.

(549) היא דיברה הרבה, אבל בעלה לא אמר מילה כל

kol mila amar lo ba'ala aval harbe dibra hi
all word he said no her husband but a lot she talked she

הערב.

ha'erev
the evening

She told me her name, but I forgot it.

(550) היא אמרה לי את שמה, אבל שכחתי אותו.

oto shakhakhti aval shma et li amra hi
it I forgot but her name D.O. to me she told she

She works for some company in Italy, but I don't remember the name.

(551) היא עובדת בשביל איזו חברה באיטליה, אבל אני לא

lo ani aval be'italya khevra eizo bishvil ovedet hi
no I but in Italy company some for she works she

זוכר את השם.

hashem et zokher
the name D.O. I remember

Should we take a taxi or just walk?

(552) שניקח מונית או שפשוט נלך ברגל?

baregel nelekh shepashut o monit shenikakh
by foot we will go that just or taxi that we will take

Smoking is prohibited in most restaurants.

(553) העישון אסור ברוב המסעדות.

hamisadot berov asur ha'ishun
the restaurants in most forbidden the smoking

So long as you have a fever, you must stay in bed.

(554) כל עוד יש לך חום, אתה חייב להישאר במיטה.

bamita lehisha'er khayav ata khom yesh lekha kol od
in the bed to stay you must you fever you have as long as

(555) Social media, such as Facebook and Twitter, is addictive.

רשתות חברתיות, כמו פייסבוק וטוויטר, הן ממכרות.
memakrot hen vetwiter feisbuk kmo khevratiyot reshatot
addictive they and Twitter Facebook such as social networks

(556) Solar panels convert sunlight into electricity.

תאים סולרים ממירים אור שמש לחשמל.
lakhashmal shemesh or memirim solarim ta'im
into the electricity sun light of they convert solar cells of

(557) Some of the neighbors are unfriendly, but most are nice.

חלק מהשכנים הם לא ידידותיים, אבל רובם
rubam aval yediduti'im lo hem mehashkhenim khelek
most of them but friendly not they of the neighbors some

נחמדים.
nekhmadim
nice

(558) Sometimes renting is better than buying a house.

לפעמים עדיף לשכור בית מלקנות אותו.
oto miliknot ba'it liskor adif lifamim
it than to buy house to rent preferable sometimes

(559) Sports are ninety percent physical and fifty percent mental.

ספורט זה תשעים אחוז גופני וחמישים אחוז נפשי.
nafshi akhuz vekhamishim gufani akhuz tishim ze sport
mental percent and fifty physical percent ninety this sport

(560) Take a couple of sandwiches with you for the trip.

קח שני סנדוויצ'ים איתך לטיול.
latiyul itkha sendvichim shnei kakh
for the trip with you sandwiches two of take

(561) Take your time. There's no rush.

קח את הזמן. אין מה למהר.
lemaher ein ma hazman et kakh
to rush there's no reason the time D.O. take

(562) Talent is futile unless you work hard.

כישרון הוא חסר תועלת אלא אם אתה עובד קשה.
kashe oved ata ela im to'elet khasar hu kisharon
hard you work you unless benefit lacking it talent

(563) Tehran has over eight million residents.

יש יותר משמונה מיליון תושבים בטהרן.
beteheran toshavim milyon mishmona yoter yesh
in Tehran residents million than eight more there are

(564) Tell me all about your trip to Japan.

ספר לי הכל על הטיול שלך ליפן.
leyapan shelkha hatiyul al hakol li saper
to Japan your the trip about everything to me tell

(565) Tell me the truth. Have you started smoking again?

תגיד לי את האמת. חזרת לעשן?
le'ashen khazarta ha'emet et li tagid
to smoke you returned the truth D.O. to me you will tell

(566) Ten percent of the population was born abroad.

עשרה אחוז מהאוכלוסיה נולד בחו"ל.
bekhul nolad meha'ukhlusiya akhuz asara
abroad it was born of the population percent ten

Thankfully it didn't rain on our wedding day.

(567) למרבה המזל לא ירד גשם ביום החתונה שלנו.
shel<u>a</u>nu hakhatuna beyom g<u>e</u>shem yarad lo lemarbe hamazal
our the wedding on day of rain it fell no luckily

That guy is strong. He lifts heavy weights and eats a lot.

(568) הבחור ההוא חזק. הוא מרים משקלים כבדים ואוכל
ve'okhel kvedim mishkalim merim hu khazak hahu habakhur
and he eats heavy weights he lifts he strong that one the guy

המון.
hamon
a lot

That is Alex. He lives across the street.

(569) זה אלכס. הוא גר ממול.
mimul gar hu <u>a</u>leks ze
across he lives he Alex that

That is totally out of the question!

(570) זה לחלוטין לא מקובל !
mekubal lo lakhalutin ze
acceptable not totally this

That store is open six days per week.

(571) החנות ההיא פתוחה שישה ימים בשבוע.
beshav<u>u</u>'a yamim shisha ptukha hahi hakhanut
per week days six open that one the store

That was a terribly awkward interaction. I'm glad it's over.

(572) זאת היתה אינטראקציה מביכה לחלוטין. אני שמח
s<u>a</u>me'akh ani lakhalutin mevikha inter<u>a</u>ktsya haita zot
I am glad I totally awkward interaction it was that

שזה נגמר.
nigmar sheze
it is over that this

That was an embarrassing situation.

(573) זה היה מצב מביך.
mevikh matsav haya ze
embarrassing situation it was that

That's a crazy story. Did it really happen?

(574) זה סיפור מטורף. זה באמת קרה ?
kara be'emet ze metoraf sipur ze
it happened really that crazy story that

The airport is located outside of the city.

(575) שדה התעופה ממוקם מחוץ לעיר.
la'ir mikhuts memukam sde hate'ufa
of the city outside it is located the airport

The ambulance took my mom to the hospital.

(576) האמבולנס לקח את אמא שלי לבית החולים.
leveit hakholim sheli ima et lakakh ha'ambulans
to the hospital my mom D.O. it took the ambulance

The apartment has one main drawback. It is not centrally-located.

(577) יש לדירה חיסרון אחד עיקרי. היא לא במיקום מרכזי.
merkazi bemikum lo hi ikari ekhad khisaron yesh ladira
central in location not it main one drawback the apartment has

The baby has such little fingers and toes!

(578) יש לתינוק אצבעות ובהונות כאלה קטנות !
ktanot ka'ele uvehonot etsba'ot yesh latinok
small such and toes fingers the baby has

The bill is due at the end of the month.

(579) יש לשלם את החשבון עד סוף החודש.
hakhodesh sof ad hakheshbon et yesh leshalem
the month end of by the bill D.O. one must pay

The bill is wrong. The waiter made a mistake.

(580) יש טעות בחשבון. המלצר שגה.
shaga hameltsar bakheshbon ta'ut yesh
he made a mistake the waiter in the bill error there is

The bird flew to its nest.

(581) הציפור עפה לקן שלה.
shela laken afa hatsipor
its to the nest it flew the bird

The book was published this year.

(582) הספר יצא לאור השנה.
hashana la'or yatsa hasefer
this year into the light it went out the book

The book you're looking for is on the top shelf.

(583) הספר שאת מחפשת נמצא על המדף העליון.
ha'elyon hamadaf al nimtsa mekhapeset she'at hasefer
the top the shelf on it is located you look for that you the book

The boss isn't around right now. He is normally in the office at this time.

(584) הבוס לא פה כרגע. הוא בדרך כלל במשרד בשעה
besha'a bamisrad bederekh klal hu karega po lo habos
at the hour in the office usually he at the moment here not the boss

הזאת.
hazot
the this

The bread is fresh and smells wonderful.

(585) הלחם טרי ויש לו ריח נהדר.
nehedar rei'akh veyesh lo tari halekhem
wonderful smell and it has fresh the bread

The car is now fifteen years old, but it still runs well.

(586) המכונית בת חמש עשרה שנה, אבל עדיין היא עובדת
ovedet hi ada'in aval shana khamesh esre bat hamekhonit
it works it still but year fifteen age the car

טוב.
tov
well

The car needs new tires.

(587) המכונית צריכה צמיגים חדשים.
khadashim tsmigim tsrikha hamekhonit
new tires it needs the car

(588) The cash register is at the front. You have to get in line.

הקופה נמצאת מקדימה. אתה צריך להצטרף
hakupa nimtset mikadima ata tsarikh lehitstaref
the cash register it is located in the front you you need to join

לתור.
lator
to the line

(589) The celebration is a good opportunity to see our friends.

המסיבה היא ההזדמנות טובה לראות את החברים שלנו.
hamesiba hi hizdamnut tova lirot et hakhaverim shelanu
the party it opportunity good to see D.O. the friends our

(590) The chair is made of plastic, not wood.

הכיסא עשוי מפלסטיק, לא מעץ.
hakise asui miplastik lo me'ets
the chair made of of plastic not of wood

(591) The child takes a short nap every day after lunch.

הילד מנמנם מעט כל יום אחרי ארוחת הצוהריים.
hayeled menamnem me'at kol yom akharei arukhat hatsohora'im
the child he naps a little every day after the lunch

(592) The children behaved very well today.

הילדים התנהגו מאוד יפה היום.
hayeladim hitnahagu me'od yafe hayom
the children they behaved very well today

(593) The city is paying for half of the costs of the project.

העירייה משלמת על חצי מהוצאות הפרויקט.
ha'iriya meshalemet al khatsi mehotsa'ot haproyekt
the municipality it pays for half of expenses of the project

(594) The closest emergency room is just one street over.

חדר המיון הקרוב נמצא רק רחוב אחד מפה.
khadar hamiyun hakarov nimtsa rak rekhov ekhad mipo
the emergency room the close it is located just street one from here

(595) The coat won't fit in the suitcase.

המעיל לא ייכנס למזוודה.
hame'il lo ikanes lamizvada
the coat no it will fit in the suitcase

(596) The coffee is very strong.

הקפה חזק מאוד.
hakafe khazak me'od
the coffee strong very

(597) The coffee machine is quite easy to operate.

די קל לתפעל את מכונת הקפה.
dei kal letafel et mekhonat hakafe
quite easy to operate D.O. machine of the coffee

(598) The communication between the departments is good.

התקשורת בין המחלקות טובה.
hatikshoret bein hamakhlakot tova
the communication between the departments good

(599) The company developed a new product.

החברה פיתחה מוצר חדש.
hakhevra pitkha mutsar khadash
the company it developed product new

(600) The company laid off many employees due to downsizing.

החברה פיטרה הרבה עובדים עקב צמצומים.
tsimtsumim ekev ovdim harbe pitra hakhevra
downsizing due to employees many it laid off the company

(601) The company offers its employees the chance to attend language courses.

החברה מציעה לעובדיה את האפשרות להשתתף
lehishtatef ha'efsharut et le'ovdeiha matsi'a hakhevra
to participate the possibility D.O. to its employees it offers the company

בקורסי שפות.
safot bekursei
languages in courses of

(602) The company pays me back for my travel costs.

החברה מחזירה לי את הוצאות הנסיעה.
hanesi'a hotsa'ot et li makhzira hakhevra
the travel expenses of D.O. to me it repays the company

(603) The company will hire three new people this year.

החברה תעסיק שלושה עובדים חדשים השנה.
hashana khadashim ovdim shlosha ta'asik hakhevra
this year new employees three it will employ the company

(604) The deadline for registering for this course has passed.

המועד האחרון לרישום לקורס הזה חלף.
khalaf haze lakurs lerishum hamo'ed ha'akharon
it passed the this to the course for registration the deadline

(605) The dentist appointment is not until the day after tomorrow.

התור לרופא השיניים הוא למוחרתיים.
lemokhorata'im hu lerofe hashina'im hator
until the day after tomorrow it for the dentist the appointment

(606) The doctor examined me but couldn't find anything wrong.

הרופא בדק אותי אבל לא מצא שום דבר לא
lo shum davar matsa lo aval oti badak harofe
not nothing he found no but me he examined the doctor

בסדר.
beseder
okay

(607) The doctor laid into me because I'm getting really fat.

הרופא נכנס בי כי אני משמין.
mashmin ani ki nikhnas bi harofe
I become fat I because he laid into me the doctor

(608) The doctor says I have to exercise, for example, swimming or riding a bicycle.

הרופא אומר שאני צריך להתאמן, למשל, לשחות או
o liskhot lemashal lehitamen tsarikh she'ani omer harofe
or to swim for example to exercise I need that I he says the doctor

לרכוב על אופניים.
ofana'im al lirkov
bicycle on to ride

(609) The door closes automatically.

הדלת נסגרת לבד.
levad nisgeret hadelet
by itself it closes the door

59

The economy is in a serious crisis.

(610) הכלכלה נמצאת במשבר רציני.
retsini *bemashber* *nimtset* *hakalkala*
serious in crisis it is situated the economy

The elevator is out of order.

(611) המעלית לא בשימוש.
beshimush *lo* *hama'alit*
in order not the elevator

The emergency exit is right here by the stairs.

(612) יציאת החירום היא בדיוק פה ליד המדרגות.
hamadregot *leyad* *po* *bediyuk* *hi* *hakheirum* *yetsi'at*
the stairs by here exactly it the emergency the exit of

The factory pollutes the river.

(613) המפעל מזהם את הנהר.
hanahar *et* *mezahem* *hamifal*
the river D.O. it pollutes the factory

The fire destroyed many houses.

(614) האש הרסה בתים רבים.
rabim *batim* *harsa* *ha'esh*
many houses it destroyed the fire

The fire was quickly extinguished.

(615) האש כובתה במהירות.
bimhirut *kubta* *ha'esh*
quickly it was extinguished the fire

The flight was short. Just under an hour.

(616) הטיסה היתה קצרה. קצת פחות משעה.
misha'a *pakhot* *ktsat* *ktsara* *haita* *hatisa*
than hour less a little short it was the flight

The flowers are already blooming. It's spring.

(617) הפרחים כבר מלבלבים. הגיע האביב.
ha'aviv *higi'a* *melavlevim* *kvar* *haprakhim*
the spring it arrived they bloom already the flowers

The food and accommodation were excellent.

(618) האוכל ותנאי הלינה היו מעולים.
me'ulim *hayu* *halina* *utna'ei* *ha'okhel*
excellent they were lodging and conditions of the food

The food is too salty for me.

(619) האוכל מלוח מידי בשבילי.
bishvili *midai* *malu'akh* *ha'okhel*
for me too salty the food

The foreign students must first attend a language course.

(620) הסטודנטים הזרים חייבים לעבור קודם קורס לימוד
limud *kurs* *kodem* *la'avor* *khayavim* *hazarim* *hastudentim*
study of course of first to attend they must the foreign the students

שפה.
safa
language

The garbage can is full.

(621) פח הזבל מלא.
male *hazevel* *pakh*
full the garbage can of

The garbage cans are blocking the sidewalk.

פחי הזבל חוסמים את המדרכה. (622)
pakhei hazevel khosmim et hamidrakha
cans of the garbage they block D.O. the sidewalk

The garbage must be taken out tonight.

חייבים לזרוק את הזבל הלילה. (623)
khayavim lizrok et hazevel halaila
we must to take out D.O. the garbage tonight

The German translation of that book is nearly as good as the original.

התרגום לגרמנית של הספר הזה טוב כמעט כמו (624)
hatirgum legermanit shel hasefer haze tov kimat kmo
the translation to German of the book the this good almost as

המקור. (624)
hamakor
the original

The glass fell to the floor and broke.

הכוס נפלה על הרצפה ונשברה. (625)
hakos nafla al haritspa venishbera
the (drinking) glass it fell on the floor and it broke

The government should listen to the people.

הממשלה צריכה להקשיב לעם. (626)
hamemshala tsrikha lehakshiv la'am
the government it needs to listen to the people

The government will surely raise taxes soon.

הממשלה ככל הנראה תעלה מיסים בקרוב. (627)
hamemshala kekhol hanire ta'ale misim bekarov
the government most probably it will raise taxes soon

The heart is a symbol of love.

הלב הוא סמל האהבה. (628)
halev hu semel ha'ahava
the heart it symbol of the love

The hotel bed was too soft for me.

המיטה במלון היתה רכה מידי בשבילי. (629)
hamita bamalon haita raka midai bishvili
the bed in the hotel it was soft too for me

The hotel is located about 10 meters from the beach.

המלון נמצא עשרה מטרים בערך מהחוף. (630)
hamalon nimtsa asara metrim be'erekh mehakhof
the hotel it is located ten meter about from the beach

The house looks like it was built two hundred years ago.

הבית נראה כאילו נבנה לפני מאתיים שנה. (631)
haba'it nire ke'ilu nivna lifnei mata'im shana
the house it looks like it was built ago two hundred year

The instructions say that the oldest takes the first turn in this game.

ההוראות אומרות שהשחקן המבוגר ביותר מקבל את (632)
hahora'ot omrot she'hasakhkan hamevugar beyoter mekabel et
the instructions they say that the player the old most he gets D.O.

התור הראשון במשחק הזה. (632)
hator harishon bamiskhak haze
the turn the first in the game the this

The internet makes my work much easier.

(633) האינטרנט מקל עלי לעשות את העבודה שלי.
sheli / ha'avoda / et / la'asot / alai / mekel / ha'internet
my / the work / D.O. / to do / for me / it eases / the internet

The invention of printing was very important for humanity.

(634) המצאת הדפוס היתה חשובה מאוד לאנושות.
la'enoshut / me'od / khashuva / haita / hadfus / hamtsa'at
for humanity / very / important / it was / the printing / invention of

The jacket is missing a button.

(635) חסר כפתור בז'קט.
bazhaket / kaftor / khaser
on the jacket / button / missing

The jacket is too tight on me.

(636) הז'קט צמוד לי מידי.
midai / li / tsamud / hazhaket
too / for me / tight / the jacket

The kids laughed at the silly joke.

(637) הילדים צחקו מהבדיחה המטופשת.
hametupeshet / mehabdikha / tsakhaku / hayeladim
the silly / from the joke / they laughed / the kids

The knife doesn't cut well. You should sharpen it.

(638) הסכין לא חותכת טוב. אתה צריך להשחיז אותה.
ota / lehashkhiz / tsarikh / ata / tov / khotekhet / lo / hasakin
it / to sharpen / you need / you / well / it cuts / no / the knife

The landscape there is very mountainous.

(639) הנוף שם מאוד הררי.
harari / me'od / sham / hanof
mountainous / very / there / the landscape

The laundry is still damp.

(640) הכביסה עדיין לחה.
lakha / ada'in / hakvisa
damp / still / the laundry

The leaves are already changing colors.

(641) העלים כבר מחליפים את צבעיהם.
tsive'ihem / et / makhlifim / kvar / ha'alim
their colors / D.O. / they change / already / the leaves

The lemonade is too sweet. You added too much sugar.

(642) הלימונדה מתוקה מידי. הוספת יותר מידי סוכר.
sukar / yoter midai / hosafta / midai / metuka / halimonada
sugar / too much / you added / too / sweet / the lemonade

The longer I learn Arabic, the better I can understand it.

(643) ככל שאני לומדת ערבית, ככה אני מבינה אותה
ota / mevina / ani / kakha / aravit / lomedet / she'ani / kekhol
it / I understand / I / thus / Arabic / I learn / that I / the longer
יותר.
yoter
more

The majority of people in the world own a cell phone.

(644) לרוב האנשים בעולם יש פלאפון.
pelefon / yesh / ba'olam / ha'anashim / lerov
cell phone / there is / in the world / the people / to most

The milk is in the fridge on the bottom shelf.

(645) הַחלב במקרר נמצא במדף התחתון.
hatakhton bamadaf nimtsa bamkarer hakhalav
the bottom on the shelf it is located in the fridge the milk

The mirror isn't hanging straight.

(646) המראה תלויה עקום.
akum tluya hamara
crooked hanging the mirror

The mountain is almost 3000 m high.

(647) גובה ההר כמעט שלושת אלפים מטר.
meter shloshet alafim kimat hahar gova
meter three thousand almost the mountain height of

The movie star has long, blond hair.

(648) לכוכב הסרט יש שיער ארוך ובלונדיני.
uvlondini arokh sei'ar lekhokhav haseret yesh
and blond long hair the movie star has

The movie was great. The actors were very good.

(649) הסרט היה נהדר. השחקנים היו מאוד טובים.
tovim me'od hayu hasakhkanim nehedar haya haseret
good very they were the actors great it was the movie

The movie was very boring and predictable.

(650) הסרט היה משעמם מאוד וצפוי מראש.
vetsafui merosh me'od mesha'amem haya haseret
and predictable very boring it was the movie

The movie was very funny. We laughed a lot.

(651) הסרט היה מאוד מצחיק. צחקנו הרבה.
harbe tsakhaknu matskhik me'od haya haseret
a lot we laughed funny very it was the movie

The music is getting on my nerves.

(652) המוזיקה מתחילה לעצבן אותי.
oti le'atsben matkhila hamuzika
me to bother it starts the music

The next tour begins in 15 minutes.

(653) הסיור הבא מתחיל בעוד חמש עשרה דקות.
dakot khamesh esre be'od matkhil haba hasiyur
minutes fifteen in another it begins next the tour

The number of participants is limited to 12.

(654) מספר המשתתפים מוגבל לשתים עשרה.
lishtem esre mugbal hamishtatfim mispar
to twelve it is limited the participants number of

The only animal I eat is fish.

(655) דג הוא בעל החיים היחיד שאני אוכל.
okhel she'ani hayakhid ba'al hakhayim hu dag
I eat that I the only the animal it fish

The operation went well. We can discharge you tomorrow from the hospital.

(656) הניתוח עבר טוב. אנחנו יכולים לשחרר אותך מחר
makhar otakh leshakhrer yekholim anakhnu tov avar hanitu'akh
tomorrow you to release we can we well it went the operation

מבית החולים.
mibeit hakholim
from the hospital

The opposite of "small" is "big".

ההיפך מ"קטן" זה "גדול". (657)
gadol ze mikatan haheifekh
big it of small the opposite

The original is for you. We keep the copy.

המקור נשאר אצלך. אנחנו לוקחים את העותק. (658)
ha'otek et lok'khim anakhnu etslekha nishar hamakor
the copy D.O. we take we with you it stays the original

The outdoor concert will be canceled if it rains.

ההופעה תחת כיפת השמיים תבוטל אם (659)
im tevutal takhat kipat hashama'im hahofa'a
if it will be canceled the open-air (under dome of the sky) the concert

ירד גשם.
geshem yered
rain it will fall

The package is ready for pickup at the post office.

החבילה מוכנה לאיסוף מהדואר. (660)
mehado'ar le'isuf mukhana hakhavila
from the post office for pickup ready the package

The pants are too long. Can you make them shorter?

המכנסיים ארוכים מידי. אתה יכול לקצר אותם? (661)
otam lekatser yakhol ata midai arukim hamikhnasa'im
them to shorten you can you too long the pants

The people are a bit different here than in the South.

האנשים קצת שונים פה מאשר בדרום. (662)
badarom me'asher po shonim ktsat ha'anashim
in the South than here different a bit the people

The people are fleeing and requesting asylum.

האנשים נסים על חייהם ומבקשים מקלט. (663)
miklat umevakshim khayeihem al nasim ha'anashim
asylum and they request their lives for they flee the people

The people are protesting against the coal power plant.

האנשים מוחים נגד תחנת הכוח הפחמית. (664)
hapekhamit hako'akh takhanat neged mokhim ha'anashim
the coal the power station of against they protest the people

The police found the weapon.

המשטרה מצאה את כלי הנשק. (665)
klei haneshek et matsa hamishtara
the weapon D.O. it found the police

The police have finally caught the culprit.

המשטרה סוף-סוף תפסה את האשם. (666)
ha'ashem et tafsa sof-sof hamishtara
the culprit D.O. it caught finally the police

The police stopped me because I drove through a red traffic light.

המשטרה הורתה לי לעצור כי עברתי באור (667)
be'or avarti ki la'atsor li horta hamishtara
in light I passed because to stop to me it commanded the police

אדום.
adom
red

64

	English
The problem is not difficult. The solution is very simple.	(668)

הבעיה לא קשה. הפתרון מאוד פשוט.

pashut	me'od	hapitron	kasha	lo	habe'aya
simple	very	the solution	difficult	not	the problem

The professor is internationally known. (669)

הפרופסור מוכר בעולם.

ba'olam	mukar	haprofesor
in the world	he is known	the professor

The repair is too expensive. I can get it done for half elsewhere. (670)

התיקון יקר מידי. אני יכול לעשות את זה בחצי

bekhatsi	ze	et	la'asot	yakhol	ani	midai	yakar	hatikun
for half	it	D.O.	to do	I can	I	too	expensive	the repair

מחיר במקום אחר.

akher	bemakom	mekhir
other	in place	price

The reporter is currently conducting an interview. (671)

הכתב מקיים כרגע ראיון.

re'ayon	karega	mekayem	hakatav
interview	right now	he performs	the reporter

The rice has to cook for about 40 minutes. (672)

האורז צריך להתבשל ארבעים דקות בערך.

be'erekh	dakot	arba'im	lehitbashel	tsarikh	ha'orez
about	minutes	forty	to be cooked	it needs	the rice

The rug is two meters long and one meter wide. (673)

אורך המרבד שני מטרים ורוחבו מטר אחד.

ekhad	meter	verokhbo	metrim	shnei	hamarvad	orekh
one	meter	and its width	meters	two of	the rug	length of

The sooner we get there, the better our chances of getting a good seat. (674)

ככל שנגיע מוקדם יותר, ככה יגדלו

igdelu	kakha	yoter	mukdam	shenagi'a	kekhol
they will grow	the more	more	soon	that we will arrive	the more

הסיכויים שנקבל מקום ישיבה טוב.

tov	yeshiva	mekom	shenekabel	hasiku'im
good	sitting	place of	we will receive	the chances

The stove was still hot. I accidentally burned myself. (675)

הכיריים היו עדיין חמות. שרפתי את עצמי בטעות.

beta'ut	atsmi	et	sarafti	khamot	ada'in	hayu	hakira'im
accidentally	myself	D.O.	I burned	hot	still	they were	the stove

The student got a good grade for her presentation. (676)

הסטודנטית קיבלה ציון טוב על המצגת שלה.

shela	hamatseget	al	tov	tsiyun	kibla	hastudentit
her	the presentation	for	good	grade	she got	the student

The students of this school wear standardized uniforms. (677)

התלמידים בבית הספר הזה לובשים מדים

madim	lovshim	haze	beveit hasefer	hatalmidim
uniforms	they wear	the this	at school	the students

לפי התקן.

hateken	lefi
the standard	in accordance with

The suitcase is much too heavy for me to carry.

(678) הַמִזְוָודָה כְּבֵדָה מִדַי מִכְּדֵי שֶׁאֶשָׂא אוֹתָה.
ota mikhdei she'esa midai kveda hamizvada
it that I will carry too heavy the suitcase

The suitcase is very light. I can carry it alone.

(679) הַמִזְוָודָה מְאוֹד קַלָה. אֲנִי יָכוֹל לָשֵׂאת אוֹתָה לְבַד.
levad ota laset yakhol ani kala me'od hamizvada
alone it to carry I can I light very the suitcase

The sweater does not fit me anymore.

(680) הַסְוֶודֶר לֹא יוֹשֵׁב עָלַי יוֹתֵר.
yoter alai yoshev lo hasveder
anymore on me it fits no the sweater

The teacher called on me to answer the question.

(681) הַמוֹרָה קָרְאָה לִי לַעֲנוֹת עַל הַשְׁאֵלָה.
hashe'ela al la'anot li kara hamora
the question on to answer to me she called the teacher

The teacher corrected my mistakes.

(682) הַמוֹרֶה תִיקֵן אֶת הַטָעוּיוֹת שֶׁלִי.
sheli hata'uyot et tiken hamore
my the mistakes D.O. he corrected the teacher

The teacher gave a lot of homework today.

(683) הַמוֹרָה נָתְנָה הֲמוֹן שִׁיעוּרֵי בַּיִת הַיוֹם.
hayom shi'urei ba'it hamon natna hamora
today homework a lot of she gave the teacher

The teacher is lecturing about the Second World War.

(684) הַמוֹרֶה מַרְצֶה עַל מִלְחֶמֶת הָעוֹלָם הַשְׁנִייָה.
hashniya ha'olam milkhemet al martse hamore
the second the world war of on he lectures the teacher

The teacher said we should re-read two chapters in the book.

(685) הַמוֹרָה אָמְרָה שֶׁעָלֵינוּ לִקְרוֹא שֵׁנִית שְׁנֵי פְּרָקִים
prakim shnei shenit likro she'aleinu amra hamora
chapters two of again to read that we should she said the teacher

בַּסֵפֶר.
basefer
in the book

The teacher's explanation is better than the explanation in the book.

(686) הַהֶסְבֵּר שֶׁל הַמוֹרָה טוֹב יוֹתֵר מֵהַהֶסְבֵּר
mehahesber yoter tov hamore shel hahesber
than the explanation more good the teacher of the explanation

שֶׁבַּסֵפֶר.
shebasefer
that in the book

The team from France was a very strong opponent.

(687) הַקְבוּצָה מִצָרְפַת הָיְתָה יָרִיב חָזָק מְאוֹד.
me'od khazak yariv haita mitsarfat hakvutsa
very strong opponent it was from France the team

The team lost only one game this season.

(688) הַקְבוּצָה הִפְסִידָה בְּמִשְׂחָק אֶחָד בִּלְבַד הָעוֹנָה.
ha'ona bilvad ekhad bemiskhak hifsida hakvutsa
this season only one at game it lost the team

The teapot is almost empty. I'll make us more tea.

קנקן התה כמעט ריק. אני אכין לנו עוד תה.

kankan	hate	kimat	reik	ani	akhin	lanu	od	te
pot of	the tea	almost	empty	I	I will make	for us	more	tea

(689)

The temperature has quite suddenly fallen below zero.

הטמפרטורות נפלו מתחת לאפס די בפתאומיות.

hatemperaturot	naflu	mitakhat	la'efes	dei	befitomiyut
the temperatures	they fell	below	to the zero	quite	suddenly

(690)

The thunder came ten seconds after the lightning.

הרעם הגיע עשר שניות אחרי הברק.

hara'am	higi'a	eser	shniyot	akharei	habarak
the thunder	it arrived	ten	seconds	after	the lightning

(691)

The topic of parenting interests me very much because I am pregnant.

נושא ההורות מעניין אותי מאוד מכיוון שאני בהריון.

nose	hahorut	me'anyen	oti	me'od	mikeivan	she'ani
topic of	the parenting	it interests	me	very much	because	that I

beherayon
pregnant

(692)

The tourist visa is valid for ninety days.

אשרת התייר תקפה לתשעים יום.

ashrat	hatayar	tkefa	letishim	yom
visa of	the tourist	valid	for ninety	day

(693)

The towels are on the top shelf.

המגבות נמצאות על המדף העליון.

hamagavot	nimtsa'ot	al	hamadaf	ha'elyon
the towels	they are located	on	the shelf	the top

(694)

The traffic light was broken. A policeman directed traffic.

הרמזור היה מקולקל. שוטר כיוון את התנועה.

haramzor	haya	mekulkal	shoter	kiven	et	hatnu'a
the traffic light	it was	broken	policeman	he directed	D.O.	the traffic

(695)

The train comes in 30 minutes. Until then, we can sit here and chat.

הרכבת מגיעה עוד שלושים דקות. עד אז, אנחנו

harakevet	magi'a	od	shloshim	dakot	ad	az	anakhnu
the train	it arrives	another	thirty	minutes	until	then	we

יכולים לשבת פה ולקשקש.

yekholim	lashevet	po	ulekashkesh
we can	to sit	here	and to chat

(696)

The universe is very large.

היקום גדול מאוד.

hayekum	gadol	me'od
the universe	large	very

(697)

The walls are very thin here. You can hear everything.

הקירות מאוד דקים פה. אתה יכול לשמוע הכל.

hakirot	me'od	dakim	po	ata	yakhol	lishmo'a	hakol
the walls	very	thin	here	you	you can	to hear	everything

(698)

The washing machine comes with a one year warranty.

מכונת הכביסה מגיעה עם אחריות לשנה.

mekhonat	hakvisa	magi'a	im	akhrayut	leshana
machine of	the laundry	it comes	with	warranty	for a year

(699)

The wheel was invented about 6000 years ago.

(700) הגלגל הומצא לפני ששת אלפים שנה.
shana — _sheshet alafim_ — lifnei — humtsa — hagalgal
year — six thousand — ago — it was invented — the wheel

The whole house smells of fresh paint.

(701) יש ריח של צבע טרי בכל הבית.
haba'it — bekhol — tari — _tseva_ — shel — _rei'akh_ — yesh
the house — in all of — fresh — paint — of — smell — there is

The window was not closed during the storm, so a lot of rain came in.

(702) החלון לא היה סגור במהלך הסופה, אז הרבה גשם
geshem — harbe — az — hasufa — bemahalakh — sagur — haya — lo — hakhalon
rain — a lot of — so — the storm — during — closed — it was — no — the window

חדר פנימה.
pnima — khadar
inside — it penetrated

The workers are striking for higher wages.

(703) העובדים שובתים בדרישה למשכורות גבוהות יותר.
yoter — gvohot — lemaskorot — bidrisha — shovtim — ha'ovdim
more — high — for wages — demanding — they strike — the workers

There are 15 boys and 10 girls in the class.

(704) יש חמישה עשר בנים ועשר בנות בכיתה.
bakita — banot — ve'eser — banim — khamisha asar — yesh
in the class — girls — and ten — boys — fifteen — there are

There are big cultural differences between the countries.

(705) יש הבדלים תרבותיים גדולים בין המדינות.
hamdinot — bein — gdolim — tarbuti'im — hevdelim — yesh
the countries — between — big — cultural — differences — there are

There are many benefits to learning a foreign language.

(706) יש יתרונות רבים ללמידת שפה זרה.
zara — safa — lelemidat — rabim — itronot — yesh
foreign — language — to learning of — many — benefits — there are

There are many famous museums in Paris.

(707) יש מוזיאונים מפורסמים רבים בפריז.
bepariz — rabim — mefursamim — muze'onim — yesh
in Paris — many — famous — museums — there are

There are many hiking trails in this area.

(708) יש שבילי הליכה רבים באזור הזה.
haze — ba'ezor — rabim — halikha — shvilei — yesh
the this — in the area — many — walking — trails of — there are

There are many social problems in this country.

(709) יש הרבה בעיות חברתיות במדינה הזאת.
hazot — bamdina — khevratiyot — be'ayot — harbe — yesh
the this — in the country — social — problems — many — there are

There are many ways to prepare a chicken.

(710) יש דרכים רבות להכין עוף.
of — lehakhin — rabot — drakhim — yesh
chicken — to prepare — many — ways — there are

(711) There are no visible injuries, but we should examine the leg anyway.

אין פציעות גלויות לעין, אבל כדאי לבדוק את הרגל בכל מקרה.

ein ptsi'ot gluyot la'a'in aval kedai livdok et haregel bekhol mikre
there aren't injuries visible to the eye but worthwhile to check D.O. the leg anyway

(712) There are still tickets available for the concert next week.

עדיין יש כרטיסים להופעה בשבוע הבא.

ada'in yesh kartisim lahofa'a beshavu'a haba
still there are tickets to the concert for week next

(713) There are three outlets in this room.

יש שלושה שקעים בחדר הזה.

yesh shlosha shka'im bakheder haze
there are three outlets in the room the this

(714) There is a detour because of the accident.

יש עיקוף דרך בגלל התאונה.

yesh ikuf derekh biglal hate'una
there is bypass of way because of the accident

(715) There is a discount for children and seniors.

יש הנחה לילדים ואזרחים ותיקים.

yesh hanakha leyeladim ve'ezrakhim vatikim
there is discount for children and citizens senior

(716) There is a great view of the city from here.

יש מפה נוף נהדר של העיר.

yesh mipo nof nehedar shel ha'ir
there is from here view great of the city

(717) There is no soap in the restroom.

אין סבון בשירותים.

ein sabon basherutim
there isn't soap in the restroom

(718) There is still a bit of wine left. Would you like any more?

נשאר קצת יין. אתה רוצה עוד?

nishar ktsat ya'in ata rotse od
it remains a bit of wine you you want more

(719) There was a delicious dessert after the meal.

היה קינוח טעים אחרי הארוחה.

haya kinu'akh ta'im akharei ha'arukha
there was dessert delicious after the meal

(720) These are my friends, so please be nice to them.

אלה חברים שלי, אז בבקשה תהיה נחמד אליהם.

ele khaverim sheli az bevakasha tihiye nekhmad eleihem
these friends my so please you will be nice to them

(721) These big trucks are used to transport goods over long distances.

משתמשים במשאיות הגדולות האלה לשנע סחורות למרחקים ארוכים.

mishtamshim bamasa'iyot hagdolot ha'ele leshane'a skhorot lemerkhakim arukim
they use (of) the trucks the big the these to transport goods for distances long

These painkillers are available only by prescription.

(722) מְשַׁכְּכֵי הַכְּאֵבִים הָאֵלֶּה זְמִינִים בְּמִרְשָׁם בִּלְבַד.

meshak'khei	hake'evim	ha'ele	zminim	bemirsham	bilvad
dampeners of	the pains	the these	available	by prescription	only

They are looking for experts in this computer programming language.

(723) הֵם מְחַפְּשִׂים מוּמְחִים בְּשְׂפַת הַתִּכְנוּת הַזֹּאת.

hem	mekhapsim	mumkhim	bisfat	hatikhnut	hazot
they	they look for	experts	in language of	the programming	the this

They both agreed to my proposal.

(724) שְׁנֵיהֶם הִסְכִּימוּ לְהַצָּעָתִי.

shneihem	hiskimu	lehatsa'ati
they both	they agreed	to my proposal

They couldn't afford to pay for a big wedding.

(725) הֵם לֹא יָכְלוּ לְהַרְשׁוֹת לְעַצְמָם לְשַׁלֵּם עַל חֲתוּנָה גְּדוֹלָה.

hem	lo	yakhlu leharshot le'atsmam	leshalem	al	khatuna	gdola
they	no	they could afford	to pay	for	wedding	big

They should exercise more. They should go walking regularly.

(726) הֵם צְרִיכִים לְהִתְאַמֵּן יוֹתֵר. הֵם צְרִיכִים לַעֲשׂוֹת הֲלִיכוֹת

hem	tsrikhim	lehitamen	yoter	hem	tsrikhim	la'asot	halikhot
they	they should	to exercise	more	they	they should	to do	walking

בְּאוֹפֶן סָדִיר.

be'ofen	sadir
in method	regular

This airplane flies directly to New York.

(727) הַמָּטוֹס הַזֶּה טָס יְשִׁירוֹת לְנְיוּ יוֹרְק.

hamatos	haze	tas	yeshirot	lenyu york
the airplane	the this	it flies	directly	to New York

This car is the safest in its class.

(728) הַמְּכוֹנִית הַזֹּאת הִיא הַבְּטוּחָה בְּיוֹתֵר בַּקָּטֵגוֹרְיָה שֶׁלָּהּ.

hamkhonit	hazot	hi	habetukha	beyoter	bakategorya	shela
the car	the this	it	the safe	most	in the category	its

This coat costs more than that one, but it's worth it.

(729) הַמְּעִיל הַזֶּה עוֹלֶה יוֹתֵר מֵהַהוּא, אֲבָל הוּא שָׁוֶה אֶת

hame'il	haze	ole	yoter	mehahu	aval	hu	shave	et
the coat	the this	it costs	more	than that one	but	it	worth	D.O.

זֶה.

ze
it

This dark chocolate contains only a little sugar.

(730) הַשּׁוֹקוֹלָד הַמָּרִיר הַזֶּה מֵכִיל רַק טִיפָּה סוּכָּר.

hashokolad	hamarir	haze	mekhil	rak	tipa	sukar
the chocolate	the bitter	the this	it contains	only	a bit of	sugar

This drawer contains paper, pens, pencils, and other things like that.

(731) הַמְּגֵרָה הַזֹּאת מְכִילָה נְיָיר, עֵטִים, עֶפְרוֹנוֹת, וְכַיּוֹצֵא בָּזֶה.

hamgera	hazot	mekhila	niyar	etim	efronot	vekhayotse baze
the drawer	the this	it contains	paper	pens	pencils	and so on

This entrance is for staff only.

(732) הַכְּנִיסָה הַזֹּאת הִיא לְשִׁימּוּשׁ צֶוֶת הָעוֹבְדִים בִּלְבַד.

haknisa	hazot	hi	leshimush	tsevet	ha'ovdim	bilvad
the entrance	the this	it	for use of	team of	the employees	only

This hotel is particularly suitable for families with children.

(733) המלון הזה מתאים במיוחד למשפחות עם ילדים.
hamalon *haze* *matim* *bimyukhad* *lemishpakhot* *im* *yeladim*
the hotel | the this | suitable | particularly | for families | with | children

This house was designed by a famous architect.

(734) הבית עוצב על ידי ארכיטקט מפורסם.
haba'it *utsav* *al yedei* *arkhitekt* *mefursam*
the house | it was designed | by | architect | famous

This jewelry was my grandmother's.

(735) התכשיט הזה היה של סבתא שלי.
hatakhshit *haze* *haya* *shel* *savta* *sheli*
the jewelry | the this | it was | of | grandmother | my

This job requires a lot of physical strength.

(736) העבודה הזאת דורשת המון כוח גופני.
ha'avoda *hazot* *doreshet* *hamon* *ko'akh* *gufani*
the job | the this | it requires | a lot of | strength | physical

This movie is more popular among men than women.

(737) הסרט הזה פופולרי יותר בקרב גברים מאשר נשים.
haseret *haze* *populari* *yoter* *bekerev* *gvarim* *me'asher* *nashim*
the movie | to this | popular | more | among | men | than | women

This movie is only for adults. It's too violent for children.

(738) הסרט הזה הוא למבוגרים בלבד. הוא אלים מידי
haseret *haze* *hu* *limvugarim* *bilvad* *hu* *alim* *midai*
the movie | the this | it | for adults | only | it | violent | too
בשביל ילדים.
bishvil *yeladim*
for | children

This music is popular with teenagers.

(739) המוזיקה הזאת אהובה על בני גיל העשרה.
hamuzika *hazot* *ahuva* *al* *bnei* *gil ha'esre*
the music | the this | popular | with | those of ages of | teenager

This new information gives me an idea.

(740) המידע החדש הזה נותן לי רעיון.
hameida *hakhadash* *haze* *noten* *li* *ra'ayon*
the information | the new | the this | it gives | to me | idea

This ointment must be applied three times a day.

(741) יש למרוח את המשחה הזאת שלוש פעמים ביום.
yesh *limro'akh* *et* *hamishkha* *hazot* *shalosh* *pe'amim* *beyom*
one must | to apply | D.O. | the ointment | the this | three | times | per day

This package was delivered to the wrong address.

(742) החבילה הזאת נמסרה לכתובת הלא נכונה.
hakhavila *hazot* *nimsera* *laktovet* *halo* *nekhona*
the package | the this | it was delivered | to the address | the not | correct

This price is only available if you buy large quantities.

(743) המחיר הזה זמין רק אם אתה קונה כמויות גדולות.
hamekhir *haze* *zamin* *rak* *im* *ata* *kone* *kamuyot* *gdolot*
the price | the this | available | only | if | you | you buy | quantities | large

This report required a lot of research.

(744) הכנת הדו"ח הזה דרשה המון מחקר.
hakhanat *hadokh* *haze* *darsha* *hamon* *mekhkar*
preparation of | the report | the this | it required | a lot of | research

This river flows into the Mediterranean Sea.

הנהר הזה זורם לים התיכון. (745)
layam hatikhon *zorem* *haze* *hanahar*
into the Mediterranean Sea it flows the this the river

This ship crosses the Atlantic Ocean twice per month.

האונייה הזאת חוצה את האוקיאנוס האטלנטי פעמיים (746)
pa'amaim *ha'atlanti* *ha'okyanos* *et* *khotsa* *hazot* *ha'oniya*
twice the Atlantic the ocean D.O. it crosses the this the ship

בחודש.
bekhodesh
per month

This shirt is not the right size for me. It's too big.

החולצה הזאת היא לא בגודל המתאים לי. היא גדולה (747)
gdola *hi* *li* *hamatim* *bagodel* *lo* *hi* *hazot* *hakhultsa*
big it for me the suitable in the size not it the this the shirt

מידי.
midai
too

This song is very well known.

השיר הזה מאוד מוכר. (748)
mukar *me'od* *haze* *hashir*
known very the this the song

This story is very famous. You have to read it.

הסיפור הזה מאוד מפורסם. אתה חייב לקרוא אותו. (749)
oto *likro* *khayav* *ata* *mefursam* *me'od* *haze* *hasipur*
it to read you have to you famous very the this the story

This sunscreen has a high sun protection factor (SPF).

לקרם ההגנה הזה יש מקדם הגנה גבוה. (750)
gavoha *hagana* *mekadem* *yesh* *haze* *hahagana* *likrem*
high protection coefficient of there is the this the protection to cream of

This sweater is made of pure wool.

הסוודר הזה עשוי מצמר טהור. (751)
tahor *mitsemer* *asui* *haze* *hasveder*
pure of wool made of the this the sweater

This tea should be steeped for 5 minutes in boiling water.

צריך להשרות את התה הזה למשך חמש דקות במים (752)
bema'im *dakot* *khamesh* *lemeshekh* *haze* *hate* *et* *lehashrot* *tsarikh*
in water minutes five for the this the tea D.O. to steep it needs

רותחים.
rotkhim
boiling

This time I want to go to an island for vacation.

הפעם אני רוצה לצאת לחופשה באי. (753)
be'i *lekhufsha* *latset* *rotsa* *ani* *hapa'am*
on island for vacation to go I want I this time

This train reaches a speed of 200 km/h.

הרכבת הזאת מגיעה למהירות של מאתיים קמ"ש. (754)
kamash *mata'im* *shel* *lemehirut* *magi'a* *hazot* *harakevet*
km/h two hundred of to speed it reaches the this the train

(755) This vaccine protects against flu.

החיסון הזה מגן מפני שפעת.

hakhisun haze magen mipnei shapa'at
the vaccine — the this — it protects — against — flu

(756) Thousands of people gathered to hear the president's speech.

אלפי אנשים הגיעו על מנת לשמוע את נאום הנשיא.

alfei anashim higi'u al menat lishmo'a et ne'um hanasi
thousands of — people — they arrived — in order to — to hear — D.O. — speech of — the president

(757) To highlight the word, double-click with the left mouse button.

הקש פעמיים על הכפתור השמאלי של העכבר כדי לסמן את המילה.

hakesh pa'ama'im al hakaftor hasmali shel ha'akhbar kedei lesamen et hamila
click — twice — on — the button — the left — of — the mouse — in order to — to highlight — D.O. — the word

(758) Today is Monday, yesterday was Sunday, and tomorrow is Tuesday.

היום יום שני, אתמול היה יום ראשון, ומחר יום שלישי.

hayom yom sheni, etmol haya yom rishon, umakhar yom shlishi
today — Monday — yesterday — it was — Sunday — and tomorrow — Tuesday

(759) Today's computers can do much more than a decade ago.

המחשבים של היום יכולים לעשות הרבה יותר מאשר לפני עשור.

hamakhshevim shel hayom yekholim la'asot harbe yoter me'asher lifnei asor
the computers — of — today — they can — to do — much — more — than — ago — decade

(760) Tomorrow is my birthday. - How old will you be?

מחר יום ההולדת שלי. - בת כמה תהיי?

makhar yom hahuledet sheli. - bat kama tihiyi?
tomorrow — the birthday — my — how old — you will be

(761) Try to save at least twenty percent of your salary.

נסה לחסוך לפחות עשרים אחוז מהמשכורת שלך.

nase lakhsokh lefakhot esrim akhuz mehamaskoret shelkha
try — to save — at least — twenty — percent — of the salary — your

(762) Turn left at the next intersection.

פנה שמאלה בצומת הבא.

pne smola batsomet haba
turn — left — at the intersection — next

(763) Turn off your cell phone before the movie starts.

כבה את הפלאפון שלך לפני שהסרט מתחיל.

kabe et hapelefon shelkha lifnei shehaseret matkhil
turn off — D.O. — the cell phone — your — before — that the movie — it starts

(764) Unfortunately he couldn't enjoy the food because it was too spicy.

כי מהאוכל להנות היה יכול לא הוא הצער למרבה
ki meha'okhel lehanot lo yakhol haya hu lemarbe hatsa'ar
because of the food to enjoy he could not he unfortunately

מידי. חריף היה הוא
midai kharif haya hu
too spicy it was it

(765) Unfortunately my bicycle broke down. I had to push it home.

אותם לדחוף צריך הייתי התקלקלו. האופניים לצערי
otam lidkhof tsarikh ha'iti hitkalkelu ha'ofana'im letsa'ari
them to push I had to they broke down the bicycle unfortunately

הביתה.
habaita
home

(766) Unfortunately, you need to wait longer. - No problem. I don't mind.

לא בעיה. אין - עוד. להמתין תצטרך לצערי
lo be'aya ein od lehamtin titstarekh letsa'ari
no problem there isn't longer to wait you will need unfortunately

לי. אכפת
ikhpat li
I mind

(767) Vacations during school holidays are always more expensive. This is the peak season.

תמיד היא הספר בתי חופשת בתקופת לחופשה יציאה
tamid hi batei hasefer khufshat bitkufat lekhufsha yetsi'a
always it the schools vacation of in period of for vacation leaving

השיא. עונת זאת יותר. יקרה
hasi onat zot yoter yekara
the peak season of this more expensive

(768) Vegetables grow especially well in this soil.

הזאת. באדמה במיוחד טוב גדלים ירקות
hazot ba'adama bimyukhad tov gdelim yerakot
the this in the soil especially well they grow vegetables

(769) Vehicle emissions pollute the air.

האוויר. את מזהמות רכב מכלי פליטות
ha'avir et mezahamot miklei rekhev plitot
the air D.O. they pollute from motor vehicles emissions

(770) Vehicles are not allowed on this street. Pedestrians only.

בלבד. רגל הולכי אסורה. זה לרחוב רכבים כניסת
bilvad holkhei regel asura ze lirkhov rekhavim knisat
only pedestrians forbidden this to the street vehicles entry of

(771) War is still prevalent in this country.

הזאת. במדינה רווחת עדיין המלחמה
hazot bamdina rovakhat ada'in hamilkhama
the this in the country prevalent still the war

(772) Washing hands is good protection against getting sick.

מחלות. מפני טובה הגנה נותנת ידיים רחיצת
makhalot mipnei tova hagana notenet yada'im rekhitsat
sickness against good protection it gives hands washing of

We absolutely must refuel. We have almost no gas left.

(773) חובה עלינו לתדלק. כמעט שלא נשאר לנו דלק.

khova *aleinu* *letadlek* *kimat* *shelo* *nishar* *lanu* *delek*
requirement on us to refuel almost that no it remains to us gasoline

We all hugged as we said good-bye.

(774) התחבקנו כולנו כשאמרנו להתראות.

hitkhabaknu *kulanu* *kshe'amarnu* *lehitra'ot*
we hugged all of us when we said goodbye

We always go for a walk after dinner.

(775) אנחנו תמיד יוצאים להליכה אחרי ארוחת הערב.

anakhnu *tamid* *yotsim* *lehalikha* *akharei* *arukhat* *ha'erev*
we always we go out for a walk after meal of the evening

We are about the same age.

(776) אנחנו באותו גיל בערך.

anakhnu *be'oto* *gil* *be'erekh*
we at same age approximately

We are leaving at 8 o'clock sharp. Please be here on time.

(777) אנחנו יוצאים בשעה שמונה על השעון. בבקשה תהיה פה בזמן.

anakhnu *yotsim* *besha'a shmone* *al hasha'on* *bevakasha* *tihiye*
we we leave at eight o'clock on the dot please you will be

po *bazman*
here on time

We are open every day except Saturday.

(778) אנחנו פתוחים כל יום למעט שבת.

anakhnu *ptukhim* *kol* *yom* *lema'et* *shabat*
we open every day except for Saturday

We are sitting in the living room and watching TV.

(779) אנחנו יושבים בסלון וצופים בטלוויזיה.

anakhnu *yoshvim* *basalon* *vetsofim* *batelevizya*
we we sit in the living room and we watch at the television

We are staying at a hotel by the sea.

(780) אנחנו משתכנים במלון ליד הים.

anakhnu *mishtaknim* *bemalon* *leyad* *hayam*
we we stay at hotel next to the sea

We bought a piece of land and want to build a house there.

(781) קנינו מגרש ואנחנו רוצים לבנות שם בית.

kaninu *migrash* *ve'anakhnu* *rotsim* *livnot* *sham* *ba'it*
we bought piece of land and we we want to build there house

We bought ourselves a new couch and armchair.

(782) קנינו לעצמנו ספה וכורסה חדשות.

kaninu *le'atsmenu* *sapa* *vekursa* *khadashot*
we bought for ourselves couch and armchair new

We came as quickly as we could.

(783) הגענו הכי מהר שיכולנו.

higanu *hakhi* *maher* *sheyakholnu*
we came most quick that we could

We can meet tomorrow, but I am not free until after noon. (784)

אנחנו יכולים להיפגש מחר, אבל אני לא פנוי עד
anakhnu yekholim lehipagesh makhar, aval ani lo panui ad
we we can to meet tomorrow but I not free until

אחרי שתים עשרה בצוהריים.
akharei shtem esre batsohora'im
after twelve in the afternoon

We chatted about the political debate. (785)

שוחחנו על העימות בין הפוליטיקאים.
sokhakhnu al ha'imut bein hapolitika'im
we chatted about the debate between the politicians

We congratulate you on the birth of your child! (786)

אנחנו מברכים אותך על הולדת ביתך.
anakhnu mevarkhim otakh al huledet bitekh
we we congratulate you on birth of your child

We decided to buy a smaller, more fuel-efficient car. (787)

החלטנו לקנות מכונית קטנה יותר ויעילה יותר מבחינת
hekhlatnu liknot mekhonit ktana yoter veye'ila yoter mibkhinat
we decided to buy car small more and efficient more as far as

צריכת הדלק.
tsrikhat hadelek
consumption of the fuel

We don't eat meat. We are vegetarian. (788)

אנחנו לא אוכלים בשר. אנחנו צמחונים.
anakhnu lo okhlim basar anakhnu tsimkhonim
we no we eat meat we vegetarian

We don't have enough space in our small apartment. (789)

אין לנו מספיק מקום בדירה הקטנה שלנו.
ein lanu maspik makom badira haktana shelanu
we don't have enough space in the apartment the small our

We got married in 1990. (790)

התחתנו באלף תשע מאות ותשעים.
hitkhatanu be'elef tsha me'ot vetishim
we got married in 1000 900 and 90

We have a nice, big vegetable garden. (791)

יש לנו גינת ירקות גדולה ונחמדה.
yesh lanu ginat yerakot gdola venekhmada
we have garden of vegetables big and nice

We have a TV with a very large screen. (792)

יש לנו טלוויזיה עם מסך גדול מאוד.
yesh lanu televizya im masakh gadol me'od
we have television with screen big very

We have been living in this apartment since 2016. (793)

אנחנו גרים בדירה מאז אלפיים ושש עשרה.
anakhnu garim badira me'az alpa'im veshesh esre
we we live in the apartment since 2000 and 16

We have gotten used to life in this country. (794)

התרגלנו לחיים במדינה הזאת.
hitragalnu lakhayim bamdina hazot
we got used to to the life in the country the this

We have great seats - middle of the fourth row.

יש לנו מושבים נהדרים - באמצע השורה הרביעית.
harevi'it hashura be'emtsa nehedarim moshavim yesh lanu
the fourth the row in the middle of great seats we have (795)

We have neither time nor money for a vacation.

אין לנו לא זמן ולא כסף בשביל חופשה.
khufsha bishvil kesef velo zman lo ein lanu
vacation for money and no time no we don't have (796)

We have no more wood for the fire.

לא נשאר לנו עוד עץ לאש.
la'esh ets od lanu nishar lo
for the fire wood more for us it remains no (797)

We have the painters in the house because we are having the walls repainted.

הצבעים נמצאים בבית שלנו כי אנחנו צובעים
tsovim anakhnu ki shelanu baba'it nimtsa'im hatsva'im
we paint we because our in the house they are present the painters (798)

מחדש את הקירות.
hakirot et mekhadash
the walls D.O. again

We have this dress in several different colors.

יש לנו את השמלה הזאת במספר צבעים שונים.
shonim tsva'im bemispar hazot hasimla et yesh lanu
different colors in several the this the dress D.O. we have (799)

We have to examine you. It might be that you have internal injuries.

אנחנו צריכים לבדוק אותך. יכול להיות שיש לך
sheyesh lakh yakhol lihiyot otakh livdok tsrikhim anakhnu
that you have it could be you to examine we need we (800)

פציעות פנימיות.
pnimiyot ptsi'ot
internal injuries

We have to go now, otherwise it will be too late.

אנחנו צריכים ללכת עכשיו, אחרת יהיה מאוחר מידי.
midai me'ukhar ihiye akheret akhshav lalekhet tsrikhim anakhnu
too late it will be otherwise now to go we need we (801)

We need to repair the roof.

אנחנו צריכים לתקן את הגג.
hagag et letaken tsrikhim anakhnu
the roof D.O. to repair we need we (802)

We have to hurry. Otherwise we'll miss the train.

אנחנו צריכים למהר. אחרת נפספס את הרכבת.
harakevet et nefasfes akheret lemaher tsrikhim anakhnu
the train D.O. we will miss otherwise to hurry we need we (803)

We have to operate on your foot immediately.

אנחנו צריכים לנתח את כף הרגל שלך במידי.
bamiyadi shelakh kaf haregel et lenate'akh tsrikhim anakhnu
immediately your the foot D.O. to operate on we need we (804)

We have to separate the garbage from the recycling.

אנחנו צריכים להפריד את האשפה מהמחזור.
mehamikhzur ha'ashpa et lehafrid tsrikhim anakhnu
from the recycling the garbage D.O. to separate we need we (805)

77

We have too few players. We need one more.

(806) חסרים לנו שחקנים. אנחנו צריכים עוד אחד.
ekhad od tsrikhim anakhnu sakhkanim lanu khaserim
one another we need we players to us lacking

We have two adult daughters.

(807) יש לנו שתי בנות בוגרות.
bogrot banot shtei yesh lanu
adult daughters two of we have

We have two trees in front of our house.

(808) יש לנו שני עצים מול הבית שלנו.
shelanu haba'it mul etsim shnei yesh lanu
our house in front of trees two of we have

We have very good working conditions in our company.

(809) יש לנו תנאי עבודה מאוד טובים בחברה שלנו.
shelanu bakhevra tovim me'od avoda tna'ei yesh lanu
our in the company good very work conditions of we have

We haven't seen each other for a long time. - Yes, that was really long ago.

(810) לא ראינו אחד את השני כבר המון זמן. - כן, זה היה
haya ze ken zman hamon kvar ekhad et hasheni ra'inu lo
it was that yes time much already each other we saw no

לפני הרבה זמן.
zman harbe lifnei
time much ago

We just sat down to eat breakfast.

(811) בדיוק ישבנו לאכול ארוחת בוקר.
boker arukhat le'ekhol yashavnu bediyuk
morning meal of to eat we sat down just

We landed two hours late.

(812) נחתנו באיחור של שעתיים.
sha'ata'im shel be'ikhur nakhatnu
two hours of late we landed

We left the light on all night.

(813) השארנו את האור דולק כל הלילה.
halaila kol dolek ha'or et hisharnu
the night all lit the light D.O. we left

We like them because they are so funny.

(814) אנחנו אוהבים אותם כי הם כל כך מצחיקים.
matskhikim kol kakh hem ki otam ohavim anakhnu
funny so they because them we like we

We live in a nice neighborhood.

(815) אנחנו גרים בשכונה נחמדה.
nekhmada beshkhuna garim anakhnu
nice in neighborhood we live we

We live on the second floor, and my parents live on the floor above us.

(816) אנחנו גרים בקומה השניה, וההורים שלי גרים
garim sheli vehahorim hashniya bakoma garim anakhnu
they live my and the parents the second on the floor we live we

בקומה מעלינו.
me'aleinu bakoma
above us on the floor

We live outside of the city.

(817) אנחנו גרים מחוץ לעיר.
anakhnu garim mikhuts la'ir
we / we live / outside / of the city

We live upstairs on the 4th floor.

(818) אנחנו גרים למעלה בקומה הרביעית.
anakhnu garim lemala bakoma harevi'it
we / we live / upstairs / on the floor / the fourth

We lived abroad for a long time, but now we are back.

(819) גרנו בחו"ל תקופה ארוכה, אבל עכשיו חזרנו.
garnu bekhul tkufa aruka aval akhshav khazarnu
we lived / abroad / period / long / but / now / we returned

We lost the last few games. Thankfully we won this time.

(820) הפסדנו בכמה משחקים אחרונים. למרבה המזל ניצחנו
hifsadnu bekhama miskhakim akharonim lemarbe hamazal nitsakhnu
we lost / a few / games / last / thankfully / we won

הפעם.
hapa'am
this time

We need a creative solution to this problem because the standard solutions aren't working.

(821) אנחנו צריכים פתרון יצירתי לבעיה הזאת כי
anakhnu tsrikhim pitron yetsirati labe'aya hazot ki
we / we need / solution / creative / to the problem / the this / because

הפתרונות הסטנדרטיים לא עובדים.
hapitronot hastandarti'im lo ovdim
the solutions / the standard / no / they work

We need another fork, please.

(822) אנחנו צריכים מזלג נוסף, בבקשה.
anakhnu tsrikhim mazleg nosaf bevakasha
we / we need / fork / another / please

We need lots of candles for your birthday cake. You are old.

(823) אנחנו צריכים המון נרות לעוגת יום ההולדת שלך.
anakhnu tsrikhim hamon nerot le'ugat yom hahuledet shelkha
we / we need / lots of / candles / for cake of / the birthday / your

אתה זקן.
ata zaken
you / old

We need the following details from you: name, address, date of birth.

(824) אנחנו צריכים את הפרטים הבאים ממך: שם, כתובת,
anakhnu tsrikhim et hapratim haba'im mimkha shem ktovet
we / we need / D.O. / the details / the following / from you / name / address

תאריך לידה.
ta'arikh leida
date of / birth

79

(825) We need three to four weeks for the renovation.

אנחנו צריכים בין שלושה לארבעה שבועות
anakhnu tsrikhim bein shlosha le'arba'a shavu'ot
we — we need — between — three — to four — weeks

לשיפוץ.
lashiputs
for the renovation

(826) We only have a small apartment, but we are happy with it.

יש לנו רק דירה קטנה, אבל אנחנו מרוצים ממנה.
yesh lanu rak dira ktana, aval anakhnu merutsim mimena
we have — only — apartment — small — but — we — satisfied — with it

(827) We own the business together. We are partners.

העסק בבעלות שנינו. אנחנו שותפים.
ha'esek beva'alut shneinu. anakhnu shutafim
the business — in ownership of — both of us — we — partners

(828) We plan to go to Portugal for our upcoming vacation.

אנחנו מתכננים ללכת לפורטוגל בחופשה הבאה.
anakhnu metakhnenim lalekhet leportugal bakhufsha haba'a
we — we plan — to go — to Portugal — for the vacation — next

(829) We really wanted to visit friends, but then we just stayed home.

ממש רצינו לבקר חברים, אבל אז פשוט נשארנו
mamash ratsinu levaker khaverim, aval az pashut nisharnu
really — we wanted — to visit — friends — but — then — just — we stayed

בבית.
baba'it
at home

(830) We received your letter dated January 3rd.

קיבלנו את מכתבך מתאריך השלושה בינואר.
kibalnu et mikhtavekh mita'arikh hashlosha beyanu'ar
we received — D.O. — your letter — of date — the three — of January

(831) We spent our vacation in the mountains.

בילינו את החופשה שלנו בהרים.
bilinu et hakhufsha shelanu beharim
we spent (time) — D.O. — the vacation — our — in the mountains

(832) We still have to discuss exactly when we're leaving and what we're taking with us.

אנחנו עדיין צריכים לדבר על מתי בדיוק אנחנו עוזבים
anakhnu ada'in tsrikhim ledaber al matai bediyuk anakhnu ozvim
we — still — we need — to talk — about — when — exactly — we — we leave

ומה ניקח איתנו.
uma nikakh itanu
and what — we will take — with us

(833) We still have twenty minutes until the plane departs.

יש לנו עוד עשרים דקות עד ההמראה.
yesh lanu od esrim dakot ad hahamra'a
we have — another — ten — minutes — until — the takeoff

(834) We took the long way home.

הלכנו בדרך הארוכה הביתה.
halakhnu baderekh ha'aruka habaita
we went — on the way — the long — home

We unfortunately can't come to an agreement.

(835) **למרבה הצער אנחנו לא מצליחים להגיע להסכמה.**

lehaskama	lehagi'a	matslikhim	lo	anakhnu	lemarbe hatsa'ar
to agreement	to arrive	we manage	no	we	unfortunately

We usually go abroad on vacation.

(836) **אנחנו בדרך כלל יוצאים לחופשה בחו"ל.**

bekhul	lekhufsha	yotsim	bederekh klal	anakhnu
abroad	on vacation	we go	usually	we

We want freedom of speech.

(837) **אנחנו רוצים חופש ביטוי.**

bitui	khofesh	rotsim	anakhnu
expression	freedom of	we want	we

We want to build a house and are looking for a cheap plot of land.

(838) **אנחנו רוצים לבנות בית ומחפשים מגרש זול.**

zol	migrash	umekhapsim	ba'it	livnot	rotsim	anakhnu
cheap	plot of land	and we look for	house	to build	we want	we

We want to buy our teacher a gift. Who would like to join in?

(839) **אנחנו רוצים לקנות שי למורה שלנו. מי רוצה**

rotse	mi	shelanu	lamora	shai	liknot	rotsim	anakhnu
he wants	who	our	for the teacher	gift	to buy	we want	we

להשתתף ?

lehishtatef
to join in

We want to give you something for your birthday.

(840) **אנחנו רוצים לתת לך משהו ליום ההולדת שלך.**

shelkha	leyom hahuledet	mashehu	lekha	latet	rotsim	anakhnu
your	for the birthday	something	to you	to give	we want	we

We want to spend the night outdoors under the moon and stars.

(841) **אנחנו רוצים לבלות את הלילה בחוץ תחת הירח**

hayare'akh	takhat	bakhuts	halaila	et	levalot	rotsim	anakhnu
the moon	under	outdoors	the night	D.O.	to spend (time)	we want	we

והכוכבים.

vehakokhavim
and the stars

We were friends as children, but we don't like each other as adults.

(842) **היינו חברים כילדים, אבל אנחנו לא מחבבים**

mekhabevim	lo	anakhnu	aval	kiyladim	khaverim	ha'inu
we like	no	we	but	as children	friends	we were

אחד את השני כמבוגרים.

kimvugarim	ekhad et hasheni
as adults	each other

We will advise you in legal matters.

(843) **אנחנו נייעץ לך בעניינים משפטיים.**

mishpati'im	be'inyanim	lekha	neya'ets	anakhnu
legal	in matters	to you	we will advise	we

(844) We'll live in this apartment for a year and then move somewhere else.

אנחנו נגור בדירה הזאת לשנה ואז נעבור
anakhnu nagur badira hazot leshana ve'az na'avor
we we will live in the apartment the this for a year and then we will move

למקום אחר.
lemakom akher
to place different

(845) We're going camping, so we're taking a tent with us.

אנחנו יוצאים לקמפינג, אז ניקח אוהל איתנו.
anakhnu yotsim lekemping az nikakh ohel itanu
we we go to camping so we will take tent with us

(846) We're going on vacation with some friends. It should be fun.

אנחנו יוצאים לחופשה עם כמה חברים. בטח יהיה
anakhnu yotsim lekhufsha im kama khaverim betakh ihiye
we we go on vacation with several friends definitely it will be

כיף.
kef
fun

(847) We're looking for an apartment in a central location.

אנחנו מחפשים דירה במיקום מרכזי.
anakhnu mekhapsim dira bemikum merkazi
we we look for apartment in location central

(848) We're now flying at an altitude of 10,000 m.

אנחנו טסים עכשיו בגובה עשרת אלפים מטר.
anakhnu tasim akhshav begova aseret alafim meter
we we fly now at altitude ten thousand meter

(849) We're putting the bookcase here in the corner.

אנחנו שמים את הכוננית פה בפינה.
anakhnu samim et hakonanit po bapina
we we put D.O. the bookcase here in the corner

(850) We're staying only until tomorrow.

אנחנו נשארים רק עד מחר.
anakhnu nisharim rak ad makhar
we we stay only until tomorrow

(851) We're taking a break once we reach the top of the hill.

נעשה הפסקה ברגע שנגיע לראש הגבעה.
na'ase hafsaka barega shenagi'a lerosh hagiva
we will do break at the moment that we will arrive to top of the hill

(852) We're taking a ferry to the island.

אנחנו לוקחים מעבורת לאי.
anakhnu lok'khim ma'aboret la'i
we we take ferry to the island

(853) We're visiting my in-laws tomorrow.

אנחנו מבקרים את החמים שלי מחר.
anakhnu mevakrim et hakhamim sheli makhar
we we visit D.O. the in-laws my tomorrow

(854) What a coincidence meeting you here.

איזה צירוף מקרים לפגוש אותך כאן.
eize tseruf mikrim lifgosh otkha kan
what a coincidence to meet you here

(855) **!איזו תינוקת חמודה**
eizo *tinoket* *khamuda*
what a — baby — cute

What a cute baby!

---

(856) **איזו סופת ברקים ! ראית את הברק ושמעת את**
eizo *sufat* *brakim* *ra'it* *et* *habarak* *veshamat* *et*
what a — storm of — thunder — you saw — D.O. — the lightning — and you heard — D.O.

הרעם ?
hara'am
the thunder

What a thunderstorm! Did you see the lightning and hear the thunder?

---

(857) **על מה אתה צוחק ?**
al *ma* *ata* *tsokhek*
at — what — you — you laugh

What are you laughing at?

---

(858) **מהן ההוצאות החודשיות שלך ?**
mahen *hahotsa'ot* *hakhodshiyot* *shelkha*
what are they — the expenses — the monthly — your

What are your monthly expenses?

---

(859) **איזה צבע אופנתי היום ?**
eize *tseva* *ofnati* *hayom*
what — color — fashionable — currently

What color is currently fashionable?

---

(860) **באיזה יום אני צריך להחזיר את הספר לספרייה ?**
be'eize *yom* *ani* *tsarikh* *lehakhzir* *et* *hasefer* *lasifriya*
on what — day — I — I need — to return — D.O. — the book — to the library

What day do I have to return the book to the library?

---

(861) **איזה יום היום ?**
eize *yom* *hayom*
what — day — today

What day is today?

---

(862) **מה אמר האיש ? הבנתי רק חצי מהדברים שלו.**
ma *amar* *ha'ish* *hevanti* *rak* *khatsi* *mehadvarim* *shelo*
what — he said — the man — I understood — only — half — of the sayings — his

What did the man say? I only understood half.

---

(863) **מה אתה צריך למסיבה ? - תכין רשימת קניות.**
ma *ata* *tsarikh* *lamsiba* *takhin* *reshimat* *kniyot*
what — you — you need — for the party — you will make — list of — shopping

What do you need for the party? - Make a shopping list.

---

(864) **מה אתה עושה למחייתך ?**
ma *ata* *ose* *lemikhyatkha*
what — you — you do — for your living

What do you do for a living?

---

(865) **מה אתה רוצה ליום ההולדת שלך ?**
ma *ata* *rotse* *leyom hahuledet* *shelkha*
what — you — you want — for birthday — your

What do you want for your birthday?

---

(866) **מה המילה הזאת אומרת ? - חפש אותה במילון.**
ma *hamila* *hazot* *omeret* *khapes* *ota* *bamilon*
what — the word — the this — it means — search — it — in the dictionary

What does this word mean? - Look it up in the dictionary.

What is the name of this river?

(867) ? מה שם הנהר הזה
haze hanahar shem ma
the this the river name of what

What is wrong? Are you in pain?

(868) ? מה קרה? כואב לך
lekha ko'ev kara ma
to you it hurts it happened what

What is your native language?

(869) ? מהי שפת האם שלך
shelkha ha'em sfat mahi
your the mother language of what is

What is your wife's name?

(870) ? איך קוראים לאישתך
le'ishtekha korim eikh
to your wife they call how

What is your wi-fi password?

(871) ? מה הסיסמה של הרשת שלך
shelkha hareshet shel hasisma ma
your the wi-fi of the password what

What kind of vehicle do you have? - I don't have a car.

(872) . איזה סוג רכב יש לך? - אין לי אוטו
oto ein li yesh lekha rekhev sug eize
car I don't have you have vehicle kind of what

What kind of music do you like to listen to?

(873) ? איזה סוג של מוזיקה אתה אוהב לשמוע
lishmo'a ohev ata muzika shel sug eize
to listen you like you music of kind what

What would you do if you were me?

(874) ? מה היית עושה במקומי
bimkomi ha'ita ose ma
in my place you would do what

When and where were you born?

(875) ? איפה ומתי נולדת
noladeta umatai eifo
you were born and when where

When are we meeting? - Around 10 o'clock. Is that okay for you?

(876) ? מתי אנחנו נפגשים? - סביב עשר. זה מסתדר לך
lekha mistader ze eser sviv nifgashim anakhnu matai
for you it works out that ten around we meet we when

When do we find out the result of the (medical) test?

(877) ? מתי אנחנו מקבלים את תוצאות הבדיקה (הרפואית)
(harefu'it) habdika totsot et mekablim anakhnu matai
(the medical) the test results of D.O. we find out we when

When Dr. Levi was on vacation, I went to the doctor who was covering for him.

(878) כשד"ר לוי היה בחופשה, הלכתי לרופא שהחליף
shehekhlif lerofe halakhti bekhufsha haya levi kshedoktor
who replaced to doctor I went on vacation he was Levi when doctor

. אותו
oto
him

When I turn 18, I'll have a big party.

כשאחגוג שמונה עשרה, אני אעשה מסיבה גדולה. (879)

kshe'ekhgog	shmone esre	ani	e'ese	mesiba	gdola
when I will celebrate	eighteen	I	I will do	party	big

When I was 15 years old, I really wanted to learn to play piano. But I had no money for it back then.

כשהייתי בן חמש עשרה, ממש רציתי ללמוד לנגן (880)

ksheha'iti	ben	khamesh esre	mamash	ratsiti	lilmod	lenagen
when I was	aged	fifteen	really	I wanted	to learn	to play

בפסנתר. אבל לא היה לי אז כסף בשביל זה.

bifsanter	aval	lo	haya li	az	kesef	bishvil	ze
at piano	but	no	I had	then	money	for	that

When I'm finished at work, I'm going home.

כשאני מסיים בעבודה, אני הולך הביתה. (881)

kshe'ani	mesayem	ba'avoda	ani	holekh	habaita
when I	I finish	at the work	I	I go	home

When should I come? Is tomorrow evening okay with you?

מתי להגיע? מחר בערב מתאים לך? (882)

matai	lehagi'a	makhar	ba'erev	matim	lekha
when	to arrive	tomorrow	in the evening	suitable	for you

When the kids are grown, we will have more free time again.

כשהילדים יגדלו, יהיה לנו שוב יותר זמן פנוי. (883)

kshehayeladim	igdelu	ihiye lanu	shuv	yoter	zman	panui
when the kids	they will grow up	we will have	again	more	time	free

When was the last time you saw your family?

מתי היתה הפעם האחרונה שראית את המשפחה שלך? (884)

matai	haita	hapa'am	ha'akharona	shera'ita	et	hamishpakha	shelkha
when	it was	the time	the last	that you saw	D.O.	the family	your

When was the last time you went to a dentist?

מתי היתה הפעם האחרונה שהלכת לרופא שיניים? (885)

matai	haita	hapa'am	ha'akharona	shehalakhta	lerofe shina'im
when	it was	the time	the last	that you went	to dentist

When we got home, the kids were already asleep.

כשהגענו הביתה, הילדים היו כבר רדומים. (886)

kshehiganu	habaita	hayeladim	hayu	kvar	redumim
when we arrived	home	the kids	they were	already	asleep

Where are you from? - From France.

מאיפה אתה? - מצרפת. (887)

me'eifo	ata	mitsarfat
from where	you	from France

Where are you spending the night? - At a youth hostel.

איפה אתה מעביר את הלילה? - באכסניית נוער. (888)

eifo	ata	ma'avir	et	halaila	be'akhsaniyat	no'ar
where	you	you pass	D.O.	the night	at hostel of	youth

Where are your so-called friends tonight?

איפה החברים בכאילו שלך? (889)

eifo	hakhaverim	beke'ilu	shelkha
where	the friends	so-called	your

(890) **?איפה אתה רוצה לשבת - בפנים או בחוץ**
eifo ata rotse lashevet bifnim o bakhuts
where you you want to sit inside or outside

Where do you want to sit, inside or outside?

(891) **איפה השירותים? - תעלה במדרגות ואז שמאלה.**
eifo hasherutim ta'ale bamadregot ve'az smola
where the restroom you will go up with the stairs and then left

Where is the toilet? - Go up the stairs and then left.

(892) **?איפה במחשב שלך שמרת את הקובץ**
eifo bamakhshev shelkha shamarta et hakovets
where on the computer your you saved D.O. the file

Where on your computer did you save the file?

(893) **?לאן לשלוח את טופס הבקשה שלי**
le'an lishlo'akh et tofes habakasha sheli
to where to send D.O. form of the application my

Where should I send my application?

(894) **?איפה תרצה לשבת? אחורה או קדימה**
eifo tirtse lashevet akhora o kadima
where you will want to sit in back or in front

Where would you like to sit? In the back or in front?

(895) **?נגד אילו מחלות כדאי לי להתחסן**
neged eilu makhalot kedai li lehitkhasen
against which diseases worthwhile for me to be vaccinated

Which diseases should I get vaccinated against?

(896) **אילו מכנסיים אתה לובש הערב? - אלה שפה.**
eilu mikhnasa'im ata lovesh ha'erev ele shepo
which pants you you wear tonight these that here

Which pants are you wearing tonight? - These here.

(897) **?איזו חולצה נראית עלי טוב יותר**
eizo khultsa niret alai tov yoter
which shirt it looks on me good more

Which shirt looks better on me?

(898) **?מי ממלא את מקומך כשאתה בחופשה**
mi memale et mekomkha kshe'ata bekhufsha
who he fills D.O. your place when you on vacation

Who fills in for you when you are on vacation?

(899) **?מי קרע את הדף מהספר**
mi kara et hadaf mehasefer
who he ripped D.O. the page from the book

Who ripped the page out of the book?

(900) **?מי סיפר לך את הסוד**
mi siper lekha et hasod
who he told to you D.O. the secret

Who told you the secret?

(901) **?מי ידאג לילדים בזמן שאנחנו בחופשה**
mi idag layeladim bizman she'anakhnu bekhufsha
who he will care for the children while that we on vacation

Who will take care of the children while we're on vacation?

(902) **?מי הבא בתור**
mi haba bator
who next in the line

Who's next in line?

Who's there? - It's me.

מִי שָׁם? - זֶה אֲנִי. (903)
ani ze sham mi
I it there who

Why are you never happy?

לָמָה אַתָּה אַף פַּעַם לֹא שָׂמֵחַ? (904)
same'akh lo af pa'am ata lama
happy not never you why

Why are you only wearing such a light coat? It is cold outside.

לָמָה אַתָּה לוֹבֵשׁ רַק מְעִיל כָּזֶה קַל? קַר בַּחוּץ. (905)
bakhuts kar kal kaze me'il rak lovesh ata lama
outside cold light so coat only you wear you why

Why didn't you come? I waited especially for you.

לָמָה לֹא בָּאתָ? חִכִּיתִי בִּמְיֻחָד בִּשְׁבִילְךָ. (906)
bishvilkha bimyukhad khikiti bata lo lama
for you especially I waited you came no why

Why didn't you go to a doctor right away?

לָמָה לֹא הָלַכְתָּ לְרוֹפֵא מִיָּד? (907)
miyad lerofe halakhta lo lama
immediately to doctor you went no why

Why haven't you been in touch for so long? Have you been ill?

לָמָה לֹא הָיִיתָ בְּקֶשֶׁר כָּל כָּךְ הַרְבֵּה זְמַן? הָיִיתָ חוֹלֶה? (908)
khole ha'ita zman harbe kol kakh bekesher ha'ita lo lama
sick you were time much so in touch you were no why

Why isn't the elevator coming? - You have to press the button.

לָמָה הַמַּעֲלִית לֹא מַגִּיעָה? - אַתָּה צָרִיךְ לִלְחֹץ עַל (909)
al lilkhots tsarikh ata magi'a lo hama'alit lama
on to press you need you it comes no the elevator why

הַכַּפְתּוֹר.
hakaftor
the button

Will it take long? - It may take an hour or so.

זֶה יִקַּח הַרְבֵּה זְמַן? - זֶה עָשׂוּי לָקַחַת שָׁעָה בְּעֵרֶךְ. (910)
be'erekh sha'a lakakhat asui ze zman harbe ikakh ze
roughly hour to take likely it time much it will take this

Will you come for a walk? - I would like to, but I have to work.

בָּא לְךָ לָצֵאת לַהֲלִיכָה? - הָיִיתִי רוֹצֶה, אֲבָל אֲנִי צָרִיךְ (911)
tsarikh ani aval ha'iti rotse lehalikha latset ba lekha
I need I but I would like to for a walk to go out you feel like

לַעֲבֹד.
la'avod
to work

Will you give me a bowl for the salad, please?

תּוּכַל לָתֵת לִי קְעָרָה בִּשְׁבִיל הַסָּלָט, בְּבַקָּשָׁה? (912)
bevakasha hasalat bishvil ke'ara li latet tukhal
please the salad for bowl to me to give you will be able

Will you help me to decorate the table for the party?

תּוּכַל לַעֲזֹר לִי לְקַשֵּׁט אֶת הַשֻּׁלְחָן לַמְּסִיבָה? (913)
lamsiba hashulkhan et lekashet li la'azor tukhal
for the party the table D.O. to decorate to me to help you will be able

Will you help me with my application?

? תוכל לעזור לי עם בקשת המועמדות (914)

hamo'amadut · bakashat · im · li · la'azor · tukhal
the candidacy · request of · with · to me · to help · you will be able

Will you please bring extra batteries for the camera?

? תוכל בבקשה להביא סוללות נוספות למצלמה (915)

lamatslema · nosafot · solelot · lehavi · bevakasha · tukhal
for the camera · extra · batteries · to bring · please · you will be able

Will you send me a postcard while you're on vacation?

? תשלח לי גלויה כשאתה בחופשה (916)

bakhufsha · kshe'ata · gluya · li · tishlakh
on the vacation · when you · postcard · to me · you will send

Winter was colder than normal.

. החורף היה קר מהרגיל (917)

meharagil · kar · haya · hakhoref
than usual · cold · it was · the winter

Wish me luck!

! אחל לי בהצלחה (918)

behatslakha · li · akhel
good luck · to me · wish

With a good education you will surely find a job.

. עם השכלה טובה אתה בטוח תמצא עבודה (919)

avoda · timtsa · batu'akh · ata · tova · haskala · im
job · you will find · surely · you · good · education · with

With a higher income you must pay more taxes.

. עם הכנסה גבוהה יותר אתה חייב לשלם יותר מיסים (920)

misim · yoter · leshalem · khayav · ata · yoter · gvoha · hakhnasa · im
taxes · more · to pay · you must · you · more · high · income · with

With cars you have to check the oil regularly.

. חייבים לבדוק שמן בקביעות במכוניות (921)

bamekhoniyot · bikvi'ut · shemen · livdok · khayavim
with cars · routinely · oil · to check · they have to

Without my family I feel a little bit lonely.

. בלי המשפחה שלי אני מרגיש קצת בודד (922)

boded · ktsat · margish · ani · sheli · hamishpakha · bli
lonely · a little · I feel · I · my · the family · without

Women are in the minority in our company.

. הנשים הן במיעוט בחברה שלנו (923)

shelanu · bakhevra · bemi'ut · hen · hanashim
our · in the company · in minority · they · the women

Would you like an egg for breakfast?

? תרצה ביצה לארוחת הבוקר (924)

haboker · le'arukhat · beitsa · tirtse
the morning · for meal of · egg · you will want

Would you like anything else to eat? - No thanks, I'm full.

. תרצה משהו אחר לאכול ? - לא תודה, אני שבע (925)

save'a · ani · toda · lo · le'ekhol · akher · mashehu · tirtse
full · I · thanks · no · to eat · else · something · you will want

Would you like some fruit? The pears look quite nice today.

. תרצה קצת פירות ? האגסים נראים די טוב היום (926)

hayom · tov · dei · nirim · ha'agasim · peirot · ktsat · tirtse
today · good · quite · they seem · the pears · fruit · a little · you will want

Would you prefer to live in the city or in the countryside?

אתה מעדיף לחיות בעיר או בכפר? (927)
bakfar o ba'ir likhyot ma'adif ata
in the countryside or in the city to live you prefer you

Would you spell your name please?

תוכל לאיית את שימך בבקשה? (928)
bevakasha shimkha et le'ayet tukhal
please your name D.O. to spell you will be able

Yesterday I deposited money in my bank account.

אתמול הפקדתי כסף בחשבון הבנק שלי. (929)
sheli habank bekheshbon kesef hifkadeti etmol
my the bank in account of money I deposited yesterday

Yesterday our new neighbor spoke to me in the stairwell.

אתמול השכן החדש שלנו דיבר איתי בחדר (930)
bakhadar iti diber shelanu hakhadash hashakhen etmol
in the room of with me he spoke our the new the neighbor yesterday

המדרגות.
hamadregot
the stairs

Yesterday there was a discussion on television on the topic of immigration.

אתמול היה דיון בטלוויזיה בנושא הגירה. (931)
hagira benose batelevizya diyun haya etmol
immigration on topic of on the television discussion there was yesterday

Yesterday we got lost in the woods. We were lost for an hour.

אתמול הלכנו לאיבוד ביער. התברברנו שעה. (932)
sha'a hitbarbarnu baya'ar halakhnu le'ibud etmol
hour we were lost in the forest we got lost yesterday

You absolutely must have the brakes checked.

אתה ממש חייב שיבדקו לך את הבלמים. (933)
hablamim et she'ivdeku lekha khayav mamash ata
the brakes D.O. that they will check for you you must really you

You absolutely must register in advance for this course.

אתה בהחלט חייב להירשם מראש לקורס. (934)
lakurs merosh lehirashem khayav behekhlet ata
for the course in advance to register you must absolutely you

You are allowed to take luggage weighing up to 20 kg.

מותר לך לקחת כבודה במשקל של עד עשרים ק"ג. (935)
kilogram esrim ad shel bemishkal kvuda lakakhat mutar lekha
kg twenty up to of with weight luggage to take you are allowed

You are here too! What a coincidence!

גם את פה! איזה צירוף מקרים! (936)
tseruf mikrim eize po at gam
coincidence what a here you also

You are surely tired. - No, quite the contrary.

אתה בטח עייף. - לא, דווקא להיפך. (937)
leheifekh davka lo ayef betakh ata
just the opposite actually no tired surely you

(938) You are wrong. Their daughter is 16, not 14.

את טועה. הבת שלהם בת שש עשרה, לא
at	to'a	habat	shelahem	bat	shesh esre	lo
you	you are wrong	the daughter	their	aged	sixteen	not

ארבע עשרה.
arba esre
fourteen

(939) You can borrow the book from the library.

אתה יכול לשאול את הספר מהספרייה.
ata	yakhol	lishol	et	hasefer	mehasifriya
you	you can	to borrow	D.O.	the book	from the library

(940) You can buy a ticket at the counter.

אתה יכול לקנות כרטיס בדלפק.
ata	yakhol	liknot	kartis	badelpak
you	you can	to buy	ticket	at the counter

(941) You can call me anytime.

את יכולה להתקשר אליי בכל זמן.
at	yekhola	lehitkasher	elai	bekhol	zman
you	you can	to call	to me	at any	time

(942) You can catch me in the office until 5pm.

את יכולה לתפוס אותי במשרד עד חמש בערב.
at	yekhola	litpos	oti	bamisrad	ad	khamesh	ba'erev
you	you can	to catch	me	in the office	until	five	in the evening

(943) You can cross the street there at the traffic light.

את יכולה לחצות את הכביש שם ברמזור.
at	yekhola	lakhtsot	et	hakvish	sham	baramzor
you	you can	to cross	D.O.	the street	there	at the traffic light

(944) You can definitely cook better than me.

אתה בטוח יכול לבשל טוב יותר ממני.
ata	batu'akh	yakhol	levashel	tov	yoter	mimeni
you	definitely	you can	to cook	good	more	than me

(945) You can delete the file. I don't need it anymore.

את יכולה למחוק את הקובץ. אני לא צריך אותו יותר.
at	yekhola	limkhok	et	hakovets	ani	lo	tsarikh	oto	yoter
you	you can	to delete	D.O.	the file	I	no	I need	it	anymore

(946) You can get a newspaper at the kiosk on the corner.

את יכולה לקנות עיתון בפיצוצייה בפינה.
at	yekhola	liknot	iton	bapitsutsiya	bapina
you	you can	to buy	newspaper	at the kiosk	on the corner

(947) You can hardly recognize anything in the photo. It's so blurry.

בקושי אפשר לזהות משהו בתמונה. היא כל כך
bekoshi	efshar	lezahot	mashehu	batmuna	hi	kol kakh
hardly	possible	to recognize	anything	in the photo	it	so

מטושטשת.
metushteshet
blurry

(948) You can open the file by clicking here.

לפתיחת הקובץ, תקליק פה.
liftikhat	hakovets	taklik	po
for opening of	the file	you will click	here

You can pay by credit card or cash.

אפשר לשלם בכרטיס אשראי או במזומן. (949)
bimzuman *o* *bekhartis ashrai* *leshalem* *efshar*
by cash or by credit card to pay possible

You can't eat the apple anymore. It is rotten.

אתה לא יכול לאכול את התפוח יותר. הוא רקוב. (950)
rakuv *hu* *yoter* *hatapu'akh* *et* *le'ekhol* *yakhol* *lo* *ata*
rotten it anymore the apple D.O. to eat you can no you

You can't read the sign from this distance.

אתה לא יכול לקרוא את השלט ממרחק כזה. (951)
kaze *mimerkhak* *hashelet* *et* *likro* *yakhol* *lo* *ata*
such from distance the sign D.O. to read you can no you

You don't have to be embarrassed. That happens to lots of guys.

אל תתבייש. זה קורה להמון בחורים. (952)
bakhurim *lehamon* *kore* *ze* *titbayesh* *al*
guys to a lot of it happens that you will be embarrassed don't

You don't need an umbrella because of a few raindrops.

אתה לא צריך מטרייה בגלל כמה טיפות גשם. (953)
geshem *tipot* *kama* *biglal* *mitriya* *tsarikh* *lo* *ata*
rain drops of a few because of umbrella you need no you

You don't need to be scared. The dog won't hurt you.

אין לך מה לפחד. הכלב לא יפגע בך. (954)
ifga bekha *lo* *hakelev* *lefakhed* *ein lekha ma*
it will hurt you no the dog to fear you have no reason

You don't need to worry about your future. Just work hard and everything will work out.

את לא צריכה לדאוג לגבי העתיד שלך. פשוט תעבדי (955)
ta'avdi *pashut* *shelakh* *ha'atid* *legabei* *lidog* *tsrikha* *lo* *at*
you will work just your the future about to worry you need no you

קשה והכל יסתדר.
istader *vehakol* *kashe*
it will work out and everything hard

You get a ten percent discount.

את מקבלת עשרה אחוז הנחה. (956)
hanakha *akhuz* *asara* *mekabelet* *at*
discount percent ten you receive you

You have given me too much change.

נתת לי יותר מידי עודף. (957)
odef *yoter midai* *li* *natat*
change too much to me you gave

You have good qualifications for this job.

יש לך כישורים טובים בשביל העבודה הזאת. (958)
hazot *ha'avoda* *bishvil* *tovim* *kishurim* *yesh lakh*
the this the job for good qualifications you have

You have misunderstood me.

לא הבנת אותי נכון. (959)
nakhon *oti* *hevanta* *lo*
correct me you understood no

You have no reason to complain.

(960) אין לך סיבה להתלונן.
ein lekha siba lehitlonen
you don't have reason to complain

You have to click the link in order to read the article.

(961) את צריכה ללחוץ על הקישור על מנת לקרוא את
at tsrikha lilkhots al hakishur al menat likro et
you you need to click on the link in order to to read D.O.

הכתבה.
hakatava
the article

You have to do it like this, not like that.

(962) אתה צריך לעשות את זה ככה, לא ככה.
ata tsarikh la'asot et ze kakha, lo kakha
you you need to do D.O. this like this not like that

You have to fasten your seatbelt during landing.

(963) אתה צריך להדק את חגורת הבטיחות במהלך
ata tsarikh lehadek et khagorat habetikhut bemahalakh
you you need to fasten D.O. belt of the safety during

הנחיתה.
hanekhita
the landing

You have to pay more attention to your health and not just work all the time.

(964) אתה צריך לתת יותר תשומת לב לבריאות שלך ולא
ata tsarikh latet yoter tsumat lev labri'ut shelkha velo
you you need to give more attention to the health your and not

רק לעבוד כל הזמן.
rak la'avod kol hazman
just to work all the time

You have to show your passport at the border crossing.

(965) את צריכה להציג את הדרכון שלך במעבר הגבול.
at tsrikha lehatsig et hadarkon shelakh bema'avar hagvul
you you need to show D.O. the passport your at crossing of the border

You have unfortunately not answered my question.

(966) למרבה הצער לא ענית על השאלה שלי.
lemarbe hatsa'ar lo anita al hashe'ela sheli
unfortunately no you answered on the question my

You immediately feel much better after a warm bath.

(967) אתה מיד חש טוב יותר אחרי אמבטיה חמה.
ata miyad khash tov yoter akharei ambatya khama
you immediately you feel good more after bath warm

You look great! Who is your hairdresser?

(968) את נראית נהדר! מי הספר שלך?
at niret nehedar! mi hasapar shelakh
you you look great who the hairdresser your

(969) You lost your umbrella? You should go ask lost-and-found.

איבדת את המטרייה שלך? כדאי שתשאלי
ibadet et hamitriya shelakh kedai shetishali
you lost D.O. the umbrella your worthwhile that you will ask

במחלקת האבדות.
bemakhleket ha'avedot
at department of the losses

(970) You may not park here, otherwise you'll get a ticket.

אסור לך לחנות כאן, אחרת תקבל דו"ח.
asur lekha lakhnot kan, akheret tekabel dokh
forbidden to you to park here otherwise you will get ticket

(971) You must absolutely watch the movie. It's fantastic.

אתה פשוט חייב לצפות בסרט. הוא נפלא.
ata pashut khayav litspot baseret hu nifla
you simply you must to watch at the movie it fantastic

(972) You must be thirsty. What would you like to drink?

אתה בטח צמא. מה תרצה לשתות?
ata betakh tsame ma tirtse lishtot
you surely thirsty what you will want to drink

(973) You must report the accident to the insurance company.

את חייבת לדווח על התאונה לחברת הביטוח.
at khayevet ledave'akh al hate'una lekhevrat habitu'akh
you you must to report about the accident to company of the insurance

(974) You need good shoes. The path is rocky.

את צריכה נעליים טובות. השביל מלא בסלעים.
at tsrikha na'ala'im tovot hashvil male bisla'im
you you need shoes good the path full with rocks

(975) You need warm clothes here even in the summer.

פה את צריכה בגדים חמים אפילו בקיץ.
po at tsrikha bgadim khamim afilu baka'its
here you you need clothes warm even in the summer

(976) You see with your eyes and smell with your nose.

רואים בעזרת העיניים ומריחים דרך האף.
ro'im be'ezrat ha'eina'im umerikhim derekh ha'af
you see with help of the eyes and you smell through the nose

(977) You should clean the wound with alcohol.

כדאי שתנקה את הפצע עם אלכוהול.
kedai shetenake et hapetsa im alkohol
worthwhile that you will clean D.O. the wound with alcohol

(978) You should follow the instructions step by step for the best results.

כדאי שתעקוב אחרי ההוראות שלב-שלב
kedai sheta'akov akharei hahora'ot shalav-shalav
worthwhile that you will follow after the instructions step-by-step

על מנת שתקבל תוצאות מיטביות.
al menat shetekabel totsa'ot meitaviyot
in order to that you will get results optimal

(979) You should never give up. There is always hope.

אל תוותר אף פעם. תמיד יש תקווה.
al tevater af pa'am tamid yesh tikva
don't you will give up never always there is hope

You shouldn't lie to your parents or friends.	אסור לשקר להורים או לחברים. (980)

lakhaverim o lahorim leshaker asur
to the friends or to the parents to lie forbidden

You shouldn't pick your nose in public.	אסור לחטט באף בציבור. (981)

betsibur ba'af lekhatet asur
in public in the nose to pick forbidden

You turn on the machine by simply pressing a button.	מדליקים את המכשיר על ידי לחיצה פשוטה על כפתור. (982)

kaftor al pshuta lekhitsa al yedei hamakhshir et madlikim
button on simply pressing by the machine D.O. you turn on

You used up all the hot water again.	שוב גמרת את כל המים החמים. (983)

hakhamim hama'im kol et gamarta shuv
the hot the water all D.O. you finished again

You want to decorate your apartment? I'll help you. We can do it together.	אתה רוצה לקשט את הדירה שלך? אני אעזור (984)

e'ezor ani shelkha hadira et lekashet rotse ata
I will help I your the apartment D.O. to decorate you want you

לך. אנחנו יכולים לעשות את זה יחד.

yakhad ze et la'asot yekholim anakhnu lekha
together it D.O. to do we can we to you

You want to have a picnic? - I think that's a great idea.	בא לך לעשות פיקניק? - אני חושב שזה רעיון (985)

ra'ayon sheze khoshev ani piknik la'asot ba lekha
idea that this I think I picnic to do you feel like it

נהדר.

nehedar
great

You were lucky that you didn't hurt yourself.	היה לך מזל שלא פצעת את עצמך. (986)

atsmekha et patsata shelo mazal haya lekha
yourself D.O. you hurt that no luck you had

You will get a replacement from our company for the broken device.	את תקבלי מכשיר חלופי מהחברה שלנו עבור (987)

avur shelanu mehakhevra khalufi makhshir tekabli at
for our from the company replacement device you will get you

המכשיר המקולקל.

hamekulkal hamakhshir
the broken the device

You will have to pay five Euro for this medicine.	תצטרך לשלם חמישה אירו עבור התרופה הזאת. (988)

hazot hatrufa avur yuro khamisha leshalem titstarekh
the this the medicine for Euro five to pay you will have to

You will receive an official invitation from us.	את תקבלי הזמנה רשמית מאיתנו. (989)

me'itanu rishmit hazmana tekabli at
from us official invitation you will receive you

(990) You will receive your pay twice per month.

את תקבלי את המשכורת שלך בשני תשלומים חודשיים.

at tekabli et hamaskoret shelakh bishnei tashlumim khodshi'im

you / you will receive / D.O. / the salary / your / in two of / payments / monthly

(991) You'll receive the final decision in about a week.

את תקבלי את ההחלטה הסופית בעוד שבוע בערך.

at tekabli et hahakhlata hasofit be'od shavu'a be'erekh

you / you will receive / D.O. / the decision / the final / in another / week / roughly

(992) Young people like to read this website.

אנשים צעירים אוהבים לקרוא באתר הזה.

anashim tse'irim ohavim likro ba'atar haze

people / young / they like / to read / at the site / the this

(993) Your apartment is very cozy. I like the furniture very much.

הדירה שלך מאוד נוחה. אני מאוד אוהב את הריהוט.

hadira shelakh me'od nokha. ani me'od ohev et harihut

the apartment / your / very / cozy / I / very much / I like / D.O. / the furniture

(994) Your breath stinks. Please brush your teeth.

הפה שלך מסריח. בבקשה צחצח את השיניים שלך.

hape shelkha masri'akh. bevakasha tsakhtse'akh et hashina'im shelkha

the mouth / your / it stinks / please / brush / D.O. / the teeth / your

(995) Your opinion is very important to me.

הדיעה שלך מאוד חשובה לי.

hade'a shelkha me'od khashuva li

the opinion / your / very / important / to me

(996) Your pants have a hole. - I know, they are really old.

יש לך חור במכנסיים. - אני יודע, הם מאוד ישנים.

yesh lekha khor bamikhnasa'im. - ani yode'a, hem me'od yeshanim

you have / hole / in the pants / I / I know / they / very / old

(997) Your phone is ringing. Are you going to answer it?

הפלאפון שלך מצלצל. אתה מתכוון לענות?

hapelefon shelkha metsaltsel. ata mitkaven la'anot

the cell phone / your / it rings / you / you plan / to answer

(998) Your teacher gave you great advice.

המורה שלך נתנה לך עצה נהדרת.

hamora shelkha natna lekha etsa nehederet

the teacher / your / she gave / to you / advice / great

You're right. I'm wrong.

(999) אַת צוֹדקת. אני טוֹעה.
to'e   ani   tso<u>de</u>ket   at
I am wrong   I   you are right   you

You're the only person that I trust.

(1000) אַת האדם היחידי שאני סוֹמך עליו.
alav   somekh   she'ani   hayekhidi   ha'adam   at
about it   I trust   that I   the only   the person   you